IT PAYS TO BE YOU

Create an Authentic Career with Emotional Intelligence

By
LESLIE JUVIN-ACKER

Published by Leslie Inc.
P.O. Box 222
960 Postal Way
Vista, CA 92083

(760) 509-5449
www.leslieinc.org
officialleslieinc@gmail.com

ISBN: 9798837354625
Imprint: Independently published

Copyright © 2022 Leslie Juvin-Acker. All rights reserved.

Photo Credits: Justin Nunez http://www.justinnunez.com | @justinnunezstudio
Book Cover, Interior, and E-book Design by Amit Dey | amitdey2528@gmail.com

No part of this publication may be reproduced, stored in a retrieval system, or transmitted, in any form or by any means - by electronic, mechanical, photocopying, recording, or otherwise - without prior written permission from the publisher and/or authors.

The intent of the author of this book is only to offer information of a general nature that may be helpful to readers. In the event you use any of the information in this book for yourself, the author and the publisher assume no responsibility for your actions or their results.

The author and publishers do not own, control, or assume responsibility for any liability, loss, or risk, personal or otherwise, which is incurred as a consequence, directly or indirectly, of the use of any of the contents of this book.

The information herein is offered for informational purposes solely. Under no circumstances will any legal responsibility or blame be held against the publishers or authors for any reparation, damages, or monetary loss due to the information herein, either directly or indirectly.

The respective author owns all copyrights for material herein not otherwise held by the publisher and permissions granted.

Table of Contents

Dedication vii
Acknowledgements. ix
Foreword xi
Creating a Career as an Executive Coach in the
    Action Sports Industry. xiii
How to Use This Book. xix

Emotional Intelligence 1
    Build Your Emotional Intelligence with the Four Cs 3
    How Emotionally Intelligent Are You?. 9
    Let Yourself Be Authentic. 13
    How to Grow Authentically. 17
    How Self-Confidence Impacts Your Career 19
    Are You Burning Yourself Out? 25
    Recognize Stress Signals and Manage Them 31
    Work with Your Rhythms Instead of Against Them 37
    Be a Leader Instead of Manager 41

Attitude 45
    Get Your Inner Team in Sync 47
    The Secret to Making Lasting First Impressions 51
    Developing and Mastering Fluency in Nonverbal
        Communication 55
    Embracing Small Victories 61
    Why Career Disasters Are Teachable Moments 65
    How Gratitude Puts You in Charge 69
    Get Off the Grid and Reconnect with Yourself 73

Personal Branding 77
    Six Personal Brand Building Strategies 79
    How Do You Know When You're Successful? 83
    Don't Tell Me About Yourself. Tell Me Your Story 89
    How Authenticity Creates Memorable Experiences 93
    Recognize Inspiration and Put It to Work 97
    The Power of Focused Intent 101

Goal Achievement 107
    Achieve Your Career Passions 109
    Set Career Goals For the Right Reasons 115
    Defining Your Version of Success 119
    Three Career Planning Mistakes to Avoid 123
    Smart Career Goals 127
    What Is Your Leadership Plan? 133
    Be Proud of What You've Done 137
    Wax On, Wax Off: Finding, Nurturing, and Being
        Mentors 141

    Three Strategies For Staying Focused on Your Goals..... 147

Job Searching....................................... 151
    The Shmooz: Chad on Blazing Your Own Career Path... 153
    Recovering After Job Loss: the Forgotten Phase of
        the Job Hunt............................. 159
    Your Job Search: Effort and the Goldilocks Effect 163
    Please Don't Tell Me You're Passionate, Tell Me
        What You're Feeling........................ 167
    Giving It All You Got When You Don't Know
        What "It" Is.............................. 171
    Make Your Own Luck: How to Prepare For Job Interviews .. 175
    Build a Winning Portfolio For Any Job and Industry.... 181
    Why Networking Is a Party 187
    Job Offers: How to Maximize and Negotiate
        Them in Your Favor........................ 191

Culture.. 197
    Culture Eats Strategy For Breakfast 199
    Three Qualities of Authentic Leaders 203
    Behaviors of Memorable and Influential Leaders 209
    To the Moon: Building Winning Teams.............. 215
    Can Your Team Work without You?................. 219
    New School & Old School: We're All Learning 223
    The Logical Fallacies of Layoffs 227

Business Ethics & Professionalism 231
    Communication 101: Follow Up to Follow Through.... 233
    Stop Being a Slave to Email 239

Conducting Yourself During Business Trips 243
The 3P Plan to Starting a New Job Like an Insider. 249
Five Ways to Make Working from Home Work for You. 255
Create a Psychological Safe Zone at Work 261
How to Survive Performance Reviews and
   Improvement Plans 265

Photo Memories. 269

About the Author. 279

Dedication

For Franck, Harper, & Donavon

In All Ways

Acknowledgements

Thank you to Chad Mihalick, the Malakye community, and my brave clients.

Foreword

My work in leading Malakye.com, the professional network for lifestyle-driven industries, created the connection between me, Malakye.com, and Leslie Juvin-Acker.

A very important part of what we do at Malakye is to share thoughts about the balance between work and life, and the uniqueness of each person's journey to achieve greatness in his or her own way.

Communicating in a way that is thought provoking and reflective for our readers requires a special talent and a special ability to engage some of the world's most unique people. Through no chance and no coincidence Leslie began providing thought, ideas, inspiration, and reflective questions in her writing to challenge our audience in the best of ways.

I'm sure you'll find what's to come in what you're about to read will leave you in a better place than you are now and open doors, windows, and paths in your mind like her work has done for me.

Chad Mihalick
President
Malakye.com

Creating a Career as an Executive Coach in the Action Sports Industry

My specialty as a career and leadership coach for the action sports industry came as an organic passion.

As a teen, action sports took me out of the confines of an unhappy family life and into an expansive, global community.

Surfing saved my mental health. It really did. My family life was in the pits. The skateboarding and surfing videos and magazines that I poured over provided me a vision of something else out there for me to imagine.

Surfing gave me the ability to drop my burdens on the shore and leave them behind in the water. I wasn't just into a sport. I was into the liberation that outdoor sports could offer. Surfing gave me something productive to do with the anger, sadness, and helplessness I felt at the time.

In my youth, action sports were marketed as "extreme sports". I just couldn't get enough of it. My brothers and I would watch skate videos when we were cloistered at home during the summers while both of our parents were at work. In eighth grade, my buddies and I would look at what D.C. Shoes were coming out with in the CCS mail order magazine before class started.

I passed out copies of *Wahine* magazine at my high school that I got from a Jacksonville beach distributor to help pump up interest in the sport for women and in the publication.

You could find me hanging around Clay Bennett's shape shop where I talked him into shaping a surfboard for me.

I loved surfing and ocean preservation so much that I started a high school surf club called the Nalu Surf and Ocean Preservation Club (N.S.O.P.C.) thanks to the encouragement of my high school marine biology teacher and mentor, Vicki Loehr.

My interest and involvement in what is now called the "action sports industry" or "lifestyle industry" suited my independent and unique energy. My interest in action sports allowed me to channel my skills in relationship building, speaking, and writing.

All of these activities served as a distraction and as a viable means out of a dysfunctional home life. Whenever I felt most alone in life, the action sports community always surrounded me and helped pull me through. Without realizing it, I developed a fierce loyalty to the people in this industry who dared to be their most authentic selves and I wanted to be a part of realizing their success.

My First and Most Important Client in the Action Sports Industry:
My Husband Franck

My professional expertise in the lifestyle industry began in 2007. I asked my husband what his dream was and he said, "To work in the action sports industry."

I asked him a simple question that he still recalls made him feel very angry with himself.

It was, "Then why aren't you doing it now?"

He felt angry with himself because he had an internship with premier French kiteboard shaper Raphael Selles, but lost hope after moving to Florida from France through an internship in the poolcare industry.

Despite his fears and having little relevant professional experience, I coached Franck. I taught him how to develop professional relationships, re-create his personal brand image, and put together a transition strategy. Most of the coaching work Franck and I did required him to get in touch with his feelings and challenge his core assumptions that shaped his own personal sense of identity.

Little by little, his commitment to his vision landed him a spot out of 500 applicants at Salomon Snowboards in Annecy, France as their snowboard and bindings product line manager. It was a dream that took three years to fulfill when he received the offer from Salomon Snowboards in 2010.

Thanks to his own commitment and passion, Franck went from an industry unknown to being a sought after product marketing guy. Professional athletes, executives, and mid-level managers were intrigued as to how Franck got entry into the industry and succeeded in growing his career in action sports. Because they, too, wanted to expand their own professional horizons and didn't know how.

Whenever business associates or pro-athletes would come by for dinner or to couch surf, the conversation always came up. His answer was always the same: "Leslie's coaching."

After several productive years with Salomon Snowboards in the French Alps, Franck was ready to move forward and build upon his industry recognized success as a product marketing expert.

Reorienting our focus back to California, I coached Franck on building his new vision. In 2014, Franck landed Nixon's men's watch product line position. This position moved us back to Southern California and the energy of opportunity electrified me.

Writing a New Chapter with Malakye.com

Chad DiNenna (Nixon co-founder) and Colleen Quigley (former Director of Digital Marketing at Dakine) supported my passion to elevate the talent pool within the action sports industry with emotional intelligence.

I explained to them the merits of emotional intelligence coaching and my observations on current leadership and corporate culture trends that affected the action sports business as a whole. Their advice and encouragement led me to Chad Mihalick, Malakye.com's owner and head honcho, who enthusiastically brought me on board to write a weekly advice column for Malakye's Picks, a weekly newsletter serving over one hundred thousand readers.

After noticing the positive reception of my articles and recognizing the value I have to offer the industry, Chad invited me to coach and speak before an audience of attendees at Malakye's Shmooz trade show job networking events. My reach within the highest echelons of the action sports industry grew thanks to this strategic partnership. The influence of my coaching has made a visible shift in its leadership and their influence on business and corporate culture.

Looking back, my favorite time of the year professionally was going to trade shows and stopping by the booths of my clients and friends. The clients that I have helped move up over the years have achieved amazing personal and professional success. At a tradeshow, everyone joins in one-place, doing what they do best, showcasing their skills and I get the pleasure of seeing them in action. It is always a gratifying experience for me.

Thanks to the Malakye's Picks email newsletter that sent my essays to hundreds of thousands of people, I have been introduced to some incredible people who have changed my life for the better. One of them was Allen Carrasco, creative director of Carrasco Creative.

Together, Allen and I created the #DRIVE web series where we interviewed lifestyle industry professionals and shared their stories. The theme of the interviews always boiled down to emotional intelligence and authenticity. You can watch these episodes on Youtube at the OfficialLeslieInc channel.

Being My Most Authentic Self in the Action Sports Industry

Adding to this success in a way that I couldn't have foreseen, word of mouth developed throughout the action sports industry among the wives of executives, directors, and professional athletes.

These women, who are amazingly gifted, talented, and spiritual, came to me organically. After seeing their husbands experience expansive personal growth and demonstrative change, they, too, wanted to participate in the coaching process. They wanted to see what was causing a powerful, lasting shift in their partners.

The patronage and support of these women encouraged me to express the intuitive aspects of myself. The use of my intuition further expanded my coaching abilities and increased the intimacy of my relationships within the action sports industry. My intuition was something that I loathed and hid about myself, but these people saw it as my greatest strength and encouraged me to express my authentic self.

Because of these experiences, not only do I know the business, the products, the sports, and the culture – I also know the people. I intimately know their personal challenges, their values, hopes and aspirations, and most importantly, their spiritual natures. Each person is unique and has something beautiful and wonderful to offer the world and they do in their own authentic ways.

I realized that helping my clients be the most authentic versions of themselves, they thrive financially, professionally, and socially. The benefits of developing a career with emotional intelligence is innumerable for everyone. By helping the people in the action sports industry, they helped me create my own authentic career. I want to pass the wisdom of building an authentic career with emotional intelligence on to you.

Helping You Create an Authentic Career with Emotional Intelligence

So, how did a girl who was empowered by action sports give back to an industry that made so many of her dreams possible? By empowering the *entire* industry - at every level, top to bottom - to remember a culture that rewards authenticity and to support every individual to express their authentic selves. My coaching work helped many lifestyle and outdoor industry professionals do work that best expresses their authentic selves.

What I love most about the outdoor and action sports industry is that it was built by people who took their own path.

These individuals built products and solutions that created a 36-billion dollar industry centered around fun, freedom, and personal expression. These people are pioneers, rebels, and tattooed weirdos (like myself) who have made products centered around their lifestyle and world vision. This spirit of business and authenticity is what I bring to my coaching practice and help other industries that I coach - like high tech, biotech and food and beverage - create that, too.

By the end of this book, you will no longer apologize for being yourself.

You will no longer hide aspects of yourself that you feel are socially unacceptable.

You will discover all the ways that you can get paid to be you and laugh all the way to the bank.

How to Use This Book

Malakye's Picks for an Authentic Career

The essays in this book are a collection of a little over one year's worth of Malakye's Picks articles that were sent to hundreds of thousands of Malakye.com email subscribers.

The contents of these essays are lessons on authenticity and emotional intelligence that I have taken directly from conversations and coaching sessions with professionals at all levels of the action sports, lifestyle, and outdoor industries.

The topics in this book are the most common experiences where professionals have to decide between repressing or expressing their feelings, emotions, and nature. Each topic contains questions to ask yourself to immediately begin experiencing a mental and emotional shift.

I have organized these topics and assembled the essays therein so that they may serve as a quick reference guide for building an authentic, emotionally intelligent career.

Read this book all the way through, or go back to it time and again when you need insights and questions that will shift your focus.

No matter what industry your career is currently based, all of the wisdom in these essays can be applied at any level and in any kind of organization. Take the insight from these articles and create your most authentic and satisfying career.

Creating an authentic career can be thought of as an extreme sport. Your career journey challenges everything you believe about yourself and what you believe is possible. So maybe you're not riding down a dangerous mountain pass or jumping from a cliff without a parachute, but you are daring to be your most authentic self and that takes courage.

This book challenges you to be the professional you've always wanted to be and to realize the power lying dormant within you.

Be the rebellious one, the heretic, the badass who does what you know is true in you.

Let your career be a fulfilling expression of who you truly are.

Make the biggest investment of your career by betting on and being your true self.

EMOTIONAL INTELLIGENCE

Build Your Emotional Intelligence with the Four Cs

I began coaching in 2008 and within the first four years of my practice, I started to see the four common habits my clients developed that took them from surviving to thriving in their careers. I call them the 4Cs.

The 4Cs aren't about having a strict regime like waking up early or eating Wheaties for breakfast. I have clients from all over the world with different beliefs, cultures, interests, and professional backgrounds and I've learned that what works for one person can be counterintuitive for another.

The 4Cs are: consciousness, creativity, confidence, and connectivity.

No matter who you are or where you are on your professional path, these habits can be employed individually and incorporated for maximum career potential.

Consciousness

Consciousness is defined as possessing an awareness of oneself and one's surroundings. Consciousness is a habit of successful people who strive to understand how we relate to the world around us.

Consciousness sets the tone of all professional relationships and business outcomes.

Consider your habitual thoughts, feelings, and attitudes towards our work and the message they convey.

Are your thoughts and discussions colored with sarcasm, judgment, or negativity? Or, are they generally positive? How you consistently perceive yourself and how you express yourself through your work reflects in your career choices and relationships for better or for worse.

Consciousness includes an awareness of what matters to you and those around you. When you are conscious of what's important, you are predisposed to keep your mind open to different possibilities instead of obsessing over one singular solution to get what you want. With consciousness you get more win-win situations.

Questions to Ask Yourself:

1. What thoughts and beliefs about my work and professional relationships consistently get the spotlight?
2. How (through words and actions) can I make my values and beliefs known on a daily basis at work?
3. What is it that I really want to express about myself through my work?
4. What do I have to offer to achieve my goals?

Creativity

Creativity is a habit that goes beyond artistic talent and having all of the answers. Creativity is a way of looking at the world with continually fresh and non-judgemental eyes.

Sometimes, work life can seem a lot like the film *Groundhog's Day*. It's human nature to get stuck in routines without carefully considering how you created them. By employing creativity, you push yourself to examine the behaviors and paradigms you've unconsciously assumed. The result is to break free from your own status quo.

Creativity is also a psychological space where preconceived judgements are pushed aside to make way for experimentation.

During coaching sessions, I challenge clients to put aside their normal way of thinking and test new ways of doing things by asking, "You've already walked down this road and found that it ends here - what if we tried a different path? What would it look like?"

Questions to Ask Yourself:

1. I know how I would historically deal with this issue. So what kind of new questions would the *new* me ask to see the problem differently?
2. Am I reacting or am I responding to problems? How can I consciously respond instead of emotionally react?
3. What are the typical options I give myself or others? What different choices can we make?

Confidence

When you are aware of and clear about what you want (higher salary, better working conditions, or work-life balance), you are likely to ask for it during negotiations.

When you know what values you believe in, you are likely to stand up for them and choose professional relationships with individuals who appreciate them, too.

When you allow yourself freedom to create without judgment, you are likely to test your normal boundaries.

One way I get my clients to develop their confidence is through exposure. Exposure is a technique that gets my clients to face their fears by taking on small, manageable challenges on the path towards their goals. Afterall, confidence isn't a result. Confidence is a way of being. Exercising confidence through exposing ourselves to new, foreign experiences is a habit employed through practice. Because, it's one thing to know what you want. It's another to face your fears and be confident enough to enter into the experiences where everything you desire can be found.

Questions to Ask Yourself:
1. What are my present work-related insecurities? How can I start small and expose myself to situations that demand I overcome them?
2. What are the top 3 reasons why I should believe in myself?
3. Who do I know that confidently does what I wish I could? What advice can they give me?

Connectivity
Successful people see connections everywhere.

They see connections between their attitudes and their interactions, their choices and the consequences, and between themselves and others. Connectivity is a habit that challenges you to reach outside of your own assumptions. When you reach outside of your own limited thinking, you can find inspiration through different perspectives and share your talents to bring joy to the world.

Consciousness is something that you can raise during your connection with others.

Do your networking partners, colleagues, and clients know your goals and intentions? When I coach job seekers and those looking for promotions, I ask them to clarify their goals on a consistent basis so that *others* can be aware of opportunities for them when they're not around. This way, you're allowing your network to help make connections for what you didn't even know existed.

Questions to Ask Yourself:

1. Who are the people in my network who can help me find the answers to my (specific) question?
2. Am I clearly communicating with others? How can I make my ideas clearer and more specific?
3. What are my most important relationships? What new ways can I demonstrate how I value them each day?

Connecting the 4Cs

Habitually employing the 4Cs takes work. It means stepping out of your comfort zone, challenging your present ways of thinking, and making connections that you have never before imagined.

Consequently, by developing mental clarity, you're opening up to new ways of thinking and creating. When you're open-minded, you're putting trust in yourself to always do the best thing and trust that life will meet you halfway. And, when you are confident, you are ready to connect deeper with others in authentic ways.

The 4Cs work no matter the professional goal. I've coached many people over the years and I've never seen two people take the same route of success. So, drink tea or coffee, wake up early or late, and do what works for you! Just be sure you are confident and clear on why you're engaging in behaviors every step of the way. However you wish to create your career and for whatever reason personal to you, apply the 4Cs and get to work.

The only way to know your future is to 4C it.

How Emotionally Intelligent Are You?

Feeling. Feeling is the key to emotional intelligence.

It's impossible to retract our emotional receptors during the process of connecting. The process of connecting with others is to understand and feel our own emotions in relation to theirs.

Feeling isn't a cerebral act. While the brain processes emotions, it itself doesn't feel them. Our emotional centers in our body-mind do. That's why we feel emotions in our body and not in our receptive faculties. Our observing faculties perceive and compute, but our hearts and bodies connect. The mood that someone emits, if we're open enough to observe it, can tell us a whole world of experience that allows us to fully understand how someone feels.

Think of emotional intelligence like this: Think of rejection.

Did you first think of getting dumped by a lover? Refused a pay raise? Denied a job or promotion? Excluded from a group?

You may not know the context of someone's situation, but boy, do you understand how rejection feels.

People with the ability to go to their feelings seem to "go with their gut", "have an intuition", or "feel in touch" with their relationships and decisions. These metaphors speak volumes on how we subconsciously connect to others and conduct business based on emotional sensitivity.

The best salespeople understand emotional power - *try the product, feel the texture, imagine the sensation of having/doing/being...*

You've heard these scripts before, but is that all there is to it? Of course not.

The ability for the salesperson to *empathize* with your sensational experience builds trust and mutual respect. Trust and mutual respect are one of the main reasons why people buy from one salesperson over another.

Shared emotional experience lets us know that we're not alone in the universe.

Shared emotional experience says, "You and I are here together in this life. If you're experiencing what I'm experiencing emotional, then we are like each other."

Emotionally intelligence permits recognition of that likeness, that camaraderie at home, with friends, and at work.

So, the moment you find yourself in a situation at work that seems awkward or upsetting, go straight to the emotional component of the situation. Allow yourself to simply feel the "vibes" to find out what the emotions are saying. You might be surprised as to what your intuition tells you.

Someone might be blasting you over a missed deadline. At first, you might think they're angry jerks. But, after a moment, that anger feels like frustration which then feels like fear. The fear might have little to do with you missing the deadline. That fear, upon asking probing questions, reveals your colleague wants to beat traffic to show up to their kid's sports match on time and is afraid of disappointing his child because, when he was a child, a relative did the same thing.

I know this example sounds like psychobabble (a lot of the stories we create in our minds are) but the feelings are real and genuine. The truth, based on all my years of experience in coaching, lies within the emotions.

Strive to understand the vast array of emotions and strive to understand the factual context of situations. Emotional intelligence pays off because not only are you able to connect with a person on a deeper level, you're able to control your own responses to what seems indecipherable.

There is a strong connection between emotional intelligence and leadership. The emotions we hide are emotions we fear of making others feel. Like, hiding fear of inadequacy because of a fear of making others feel insecure. This frequently happens with managers.

All of this might seem mysterious, but it's not. Humans, while seemingly complex in our ways, are simple creatures. Human behaviors are boring and predictable most of the time.

Why were Shakespeare's plays so fascinating? Drama is built upon unsettled emotions and inner conflict. Imagine, if Romeo and Juliet's parents had a little more empathy and emotional intelligence, the "star-crossed lovers" probably would have just carried on and broken up six months later like most bored teenagers do. But where's the drama in that?

Which leads me to my final point: Leaders are in position to create harmony.

Emotional intelligence is the key to creating harmony in the workplace.

Understanding our own feelings and recognizing them is the bridge to connecting with others. Know how someone feels and let them know that they're not alone in that feeling.

Questions to Ask Yourself:

1. Thinking of basic emotions, do I know what sadness, happiness, joy, fear, rejection, shame, and grief feel like? Am I able to recall a moment in which I felt this way? Can I recognize these emotions in others?

2. Referring back to a stressful or confusing moment I've experienced at work, can I remember what the basic emotions were that underlie the experience? What can those emotions tell me about what was actually happening?

3. Do I feed off unresolved emotions in an attempt to control a situation? What would happen if we dealt with the discomfort right away?

4. Going back to the last time I was upset about something at work, was I really upset about what happened or was there something deeper lurking beneath the surface?

5. Do I allow myself to gain wisdom and insight from my feelings and those that I feel from others? If not, why? If so, what wisdom have I gained about my relationships?

Let Yourself Be Authentic

Many of us start our routine everyday at the crack of dawn to the sound of an alarm clock, or, if you're like me, have been jumped on by a bubbly toddler.

Eventually, we find ourselves in a rut and feel that we need to break free of the routine.

The thing is, hard workers have a tendency to make the idea of taking vacations and breaks such a faraway thing.

That, someday, when the work is done, when you've got enough resources, and should someone *give you the permission*, you'll be free to let go and enjoy yourself.

Whose permission are you waiting for, anyway? Your bosses'? Your families? Your finances?

Take a moment to think about the concept of permission.

I mean, *really* open your mind and let it sink in.

How much permission do you give yourself to be playful? When did being so serious become such a *serious* thing?

It's like you've gotten stuck in your roles as professional (and adults, for that matter) and, like a grinning chimpanzee, it's suddenly undignified to demonstrate an inkling of playfulness.

You walk around with a poker face all the time at work and suddenly, you feel like your whole life is a game of poker: Hold a straight face, keep your cards close to your chest, and definitely don't make any sudden moves.

Goodness, that's exhausting and a drag!

So, what do you do when your company hosts a party? Maybe you go nuts. May you get blasted and say things you'll regret because you don't have the tact or the guts to say them while sober, and you go over the limit because, "*Hey, I've been given the permission to let loose!*"

I've seen senior level executives hold straight faces even in the most benign contexts. See a subordinate enjoying the company of their wife or kids during a break? Continue acting like a robot devoid of feeling when acknowledging their presence.

See a colleague on the beach over the weekend? Just continue walking past them because, "*I don't know them as people outside of work.*"

Or, end up at a personal occasion at which a subordinate in another department is also invited? You say to yourself, "*I don't want to get emotionally close because I might have to fire them.*"

I've heard my fair share of excuses like that. It's petty stuff, but it's the experience of many because they've gotten so stuck in work mode that any semblance of play and genuine expression of joy, happiness, and pleasure have become signs of weakness.

Acting naturally is not a sign of weakness.

Some of the most compelling and charismatic leaders have a great sense of humor. And they know how to relate to others, not just as employees or consumers, but as people. People like the Dalai Lama take their work about spreading the word of enlightenment seriously, but if you've watched your fair share of documentaries about him (or met him in person), he spends most of his time cracking jokes. If His Holiness can let loose, then so can we.

Laughing and recreation (as defined as mental, spiritual, and physical expression) is good for our health. Personal expression is not something we have to wait for nor does expression exist beyond our reach. Working hard *can* involve *playing* at the same time. You don't have to stop feeling like a playful and emotionally creative person just because you are *on the job.*

Dr. Patch Adams shows us that even though providing medical attention to sick children is a serious business, humor and laughter while on the job are critical aspects to treating and healing the psyche. Which leads me to ask: what kind of bedside manner do you have on the job and in life?

Emotional vulnerability needn't be an embarrassing experience reserved for the moment after we clock out. You can actually permit yourself to take pleasure in the small moments and big accomplishments and make a joyful occasion out of everything that you experience - no matter how tough they appear to be. It's ok to say, *I'm having a human experience, I have feelings - good ones, actually - and I'd like to demonstrate and share my joy.*

Those who are aware of their feelings are in a position to control their experiences. So, instead of making a mere semblance of control, why not allow yourself to fully experience the full range of emotion at work (especially the good feelings) and be a master of them all?

Many who project the image of always working hard are actually afraid of the perceived vulnerability that results from expressing emotional authenticity. After a while, putting on a front leads to ruts and burnout - and, believe it or not, I've coached quite a few burnouts.

I'm not advising emotional recklessness and insensitivity to others' feelings in exchange for our own emotional authenticity. I'm just saying, as hard as we work, it's okay to be as happy and free to enjoy what we're doing when we're doing it. Yes, it's work, but working doesn't have to be *work.*

Enjoying yourself at work and permitting yourself to be as authentic and genuine as possible about your passions, your feelings, and joys can take on subtle forms, and can have oh-so powerful results. People love being around other people who are happy, emotionally intelligent, and can put aside their facades in order to be fully engaged in the moment. It's these kinds of people who seem to magically attract good things and "luck."

Go ahead and allow yourself to enjoy what you're doing and be surprised as to how creative and responsive this joy can make you feel. There is no need to clock-out to have a good time; the time is now.

Questions to Ask Yourself:

1. Do I try to act serious at work? Have I become attached to the "serious guy" role?

2. When I want to connect with a colleague or subordinate in a personal way, do I hold back for fear of some arbitrary story I tell myself?

3. Do I get too caught up in the illusion of job titles? Do I allow this illusion to create a barrier between me and the potential fun I can have with my colleagues?

4. What do I have to lose by giving myself permission to have fun at work? Do I see work as *work?*

5. Do I wait for the end of the day to allow myself to have fun? What are the small pleasures that I find at work and how can I expand on them to give joy to the other mundane/serious things I do?

6. Do I allow myself to be emotionally expressive and authentic? Do I try to hold a poker face out of fear of judgment?

How to Grow Authentically

Who is to say we've got to follow "the rules" all of the time?

Life is an adventure and every generation is a deviation from the "norm."

When keeping it fresh, think about releasing your inner rebel - even if it makes *you* uncomfortable.

Everyone is growing and taking paths that are right for each of us. Sometimes, though, we think we know what's right for us *all of the time* even to the point of uncomfortable comfort.

Have you ever heard someone say, "I know what's right for me and there's no way that I could do anything else differently,"?

Have you ever tried something totally new, something totally unlike yourself and realized, "This is *so* me!"?

Since we're in a constant state of change (just ask every cell in your body) who knows what new habit or belief would suit us next?

We allow ourselves to get stuck in ruts - even when they hold us back from success - just because we *assume* what's right for us.

I'm wary of people's well-meaning, but misguided advice that discourages people to challenge who they perceive themselves to be simply because it's not within their "values".

What a minute.

What *are* your values then? What *are* your beliefs?

Beliefs are not the same as values. Beliefs are changeable, whereas values are immutable. Examine what beliefs you're stuck on and understand why you're feeling stuck in your career.

Being flexible in your core beliefs in relation to your value system is the first step towards keeping it fresh. Ideas get old and paradigms shift and as a consequence, our behaviors and choices do, too.

If you literally have a different body on a regular basis as a result of your cells changing, then couldn't it be totally plausible that your tastes, beliefs, and thoughts could change, dare I say, *upgrade*, too?

It's in our nature to change into higher versions of ourselves.

Our bodies literally work to keep themselves fresh (even if we conspire against our own health with false beliefs). Then why can't our tastes and pleasures - and, ultimately, our definition of who we are and what we are capable of doing - change?

Like trying and falling in love with a passion for the first time, so do we find ourselves enjoying life in all new ways. The capacity to enjoy life in new ways doesn't lie within new circumstances or changing events. Rather, it's our own personal imagination that says it's ok to fall in love with our personal and professional means of expression like the first time but for the thousandth time in a different way.

Questions to Ask Yourself:

1. What am I forcing myself to believe that's keeping me from evolving?
2. What if I challenged and maybe changed or even abandoned this belief about myself and/or the world? How would I act differently if this belief simply didn't matter anymore?
3. *Most importantly:* How well do I know myself compared to my belief system? Do I know myself outside of my belief system?

How Self-Confidence Impacts Your Career

Self-confidence is more than presence.

Self-confidence is not just a way of carrying yourself.

Self-confidence reveals how you see yourself and communicate with yourself.

Self-confidence can be broken down by *confidence in oneself.* To confide in oneself, more specifically. And, ultimately, to trust oneself. The impact of self-confidence on the career is multi-faceted.

Faith in oneself is translated to salary negotiation, entrepreneurial risk taking, merchandising, product planning, marketing, and all other aspects of business management. Once all of the external considerations have been taken into account, the common denominator of how confident one is in their own abilities is the ultimate deciding and driving factor of entrepreneurs everywhere.

Transworld Magazine and *Tracker Trucks* cofounder, Larry Balma's recent book, *Tracker: 40 Years of Skateboard History* features an interview with Henry Hester, former pro slalom racer for G&S and owner of Swami's Cab in Encinitas had to say this about regrets and self-confidence,

> I feel like it was a personal mistake not to have started a company like my friend Tom Sims. I probably could have started Hester Skateboards or some sort of company and done pretty well with it. I have a good business sense, but I just never really felt confident that I could do that, which was a giant mistake in my life. The message to anyone who reads this would be that if the doors open, go through them, because if you don't, you'll regret it for the rest of your life...I thought I wasn't savvy enough. Now I realize I could have done that. (Balma, 2015, p.58)

With painful lessons taken into account, one realizes how banal the concept of self-confidence may be. We all talk about it, but do we really know what it means to be fully connected with oneself so that we can take big risks?

I ask my clients, some of them in the C-suite of hundred million dollar companies, "What do you need?"

What a simple and almost stupid question. And yet, it is surprisingly profound.

The most common answer is, "I don't know."

When it comes to making business decisions, sticking to your guns, negotiating contracts, and putting out fires, the most fundamental question is: *What* do I need right now?

The answer to this question is always dumbfoundingly clear. And yet, this question demands bold action and a confident inner voice.

When working in a fast paced world, we err to believe that to be self-confident is to rush into action.

As Shakespeare once wrote, *"Wisely and slow; they stumble that run fast."*

What do you do in times that require snap decisions and quick thinking? You look everywhere else except within. You ignore your inner voice, your own internal compass, and that truth you intuitively know but choose to ignore.

And what happens? You pay the price of not believing *in* yourself, but also not *believing* your inner voice. You fail. And, as a result, you must learn from mistakes instead of thoughtful and calculated successes.

One of the most impactful (and financially fruitful) ways of exercising self-confidence is through negotiation.

There are two facets of negotiations:

1. To know the external conditions of the market and,
2. To know one's value therein.

It doesn't require a genius to know what's happening in the business environment and job market. With some research, you can get a good picture of the job market based on how the market is moving. However, it takes high self-esteem to know one's value, market position, and bargaining strength in these markets.

When it comes to salary negotiations, many employers are hedging their bets that you don't understand and know what's happening in the industry and your own worth. Your ignorance allows managers driven by greed to get more work from you for less the amount they're actually willing to pay for your services or products. When it comes to salary negotiations a little self-confidence goes a long way.

I coach my clients to carefully consider these facets and to know what they personally, financially, and emotionally need to get out of negotiations by listening to their own intuition. When these components have been identified, it takes conviction and unwavering belief in yourself to know, no matter how negotiations go, that your needs will be met one way or another.

Knowledge of the market, identifying your own needs and having a high self-esteem alleviates the risk factors associated with negotiations. Because you know, in principle and in truth, what truly belongs to you cannot be lost or taken away. It takes a wiser sort to acknowledge one's own needs and to believe their fulfillment is certain. In addition, it takes a brave and courageous lot to believe in one's own nature and capacity to execute it.

Quoting Shakespeare once more, "To thine own self be true, and it must follow, as the night the day, thou canst not then be false to any man."

In simpler terms, if you're true to yourself, then you'll always be honest with others and this is where authenticity in leadership, in branding, and storytelling begins: your own intangible truth. And, when you act on the truth of your nature, self-confidence is inevitably conveyed in everything you do and in everything you make.

Questions to Ask Yourself:

1. Am I true to myself? Do I trust myself and my ability to regulate my emotions, attitudes, and behaviors?

2. Do I let others tell me what I am worth? Or, do I decide for myself what I am worth?

3. Do I know what makes me special and unique and worth investing in? Can I clearly and articulately express the value that I create in my world?

4. Do I lack self-confidence? Do I need to work on trusting myself and believing in my ability to create the world of my dreams?

5. What decisions can I make right now that will increase my self confidence? Do I have a negative voice in my head that tells me that I'm unworthy? How can I change that script?

Are You Burning Yourself Out?

Life isn't a race.

The goal is not to rush to our graves. And we should remember that when considering how we work.

Instead of trying to get there first, be there faster, or do "it" better than our competitors, what if, instead, we listened to our natural pace and paid more attention to *how* we're working instead of how much and how fast?

How can we avoid burnout while assuring that we won't be outworked?

My high school economics teacher, who looked oddly similar to *The Simpsons* character Ned Flanders, shared a metaphorical story of the concept of Diminishing Marginal Utility (DMU).

He told the story like this:

> One day, there was an ice cream man who sold ice cream to kids after school. The kids loved his brand of ice cream, pestering him for free popsicles everyday, and so he came up with a proposal.

The icecream man said, "If you can eat 100 popsicles without stopping, I'll give them to you all for free - and for ever after. If you can't then you'll have to pay for every one of them you ate."

Since it was after school, the kids were famished and knew they could beat the old man at his own game. They accepted his challenge and one by one, they greedily ate the popsicles. After the tenth popsicle, the kids enjoyed the popsicles they loved less and less, but they continued eating to spite the old man until they couldn't any more.

Only one of the kids made it to 99 popsicles, but he couldn't stand them anymore. He quit the challenge with just one frozen pop left. His belly ached and he no longer desired anymore popsicles. In fact, he was sick of looking at the popsicles! And with certain defeat, the kids handed over their money to the old man who was satisfied with the outcome.

While counting their dollars the man asked the kids, "Do you have anything left to say?"

In spiteful resignation, all the kids could say was, "DM U!"

I have always remembered this clever story not just for its benefit for teaching diminishing marginal utility, but as a metaphor for burn out. You may love your job, but doing it too much and too intensely can make you hate it.

For salaried and shift workers alike, burnout is a serious problem that affects long term productivity. There have been several studies on productivity that show how, after a certain amount of hours worked, an individual is no more productive than working a lesser amount of time.[1]

From my executive coaching experience, my mid-level to executive clients work, on average, 60 hours per week. They travel away from home, on average, three months out of the year, and many of them show up at work or work from home (on an off day) six days per week.

Surprisingly, the culprit is not the *amount* of time they work, it's the *intensity* of stress at a *sustained* level that causes burnout.

Emotional and physical burnout festers into resentment and resentment leads to resignation, thereby bringing productivity for both the employer and employee to a grinding halt.

When it comes to the "rat race", create a level of harmony between active periods and restful periods. Both are equally important factors for performance.

A friend of mine is a retired Formula 1 tire engineer for Ferrari and I always think about the tires analogy when it comes to high performance professionals: After a certain amount of laps around the track, you'll need to make a pit stop and change tires. Ignore the signs of wear and tear and suffer the consequences of poor performance. Ignore them altogether and you'll guarantee that you'll careen out of the race.

Managing stress levels through recognizing what I call "Stress Signals" (physical and emotional signs that indicate high levels of stress) and counter balancing them with another term I call "Energizers" (activities to bring the body and mind into a relaxed, receptive state) balances the times of activity with those of rest.

---

[1] http://cs.stanford.edu/people/eroberts/cs181/projects/crunchmode/econ-hours-productivity.html

Athletes know that rest and relaxation serve an important part of physical performance and endurance and integrate this aspect of "work" into their strategy.

PRO-TIP: If you're experiencing symptoms that indicate a stressful emotional or physical state, then it's time to put the phone down and step away from the work. It'll be there when you get back and it certainly doesn't mean you love it any less. It just means that the work, just as much as you, won't get any better if you keep forcing it.

Stopping a behavior, taking a break, or simply temporarily shifting attention doesn't mean that you've stopped working - it's that you're "working" on yourself so the work you produce can be just as great.

Sustained periods of stress and intense work schedules cause more than poor productivity, they degrade corporate culture through disintegrating rapport and relations.

Growth is inevitable. It just happens when you least expect it. So, forcing high performance all of the time to "assure" growth happens is not only futile but demonstrates a poor understanding of sustainability.

At what point do we get sick and tired of our work and say to ourselves, "I need a break!"?

Do you force yourself to keep going until burnout happens *OR* do you listen to your own intuition that says to pull back not just for the sake of yourself, but for the sake of the work you do?

And, if you get so disturbed about your work habits that you can't take it anymore you'll end up believing that you hate your work, failing to recognize the stress levels that got you to that point. It's at this point when you give up and when others start to outwork you. Don't go there.

It's not a race to get it all done. Take a pit stop and change your tires when you need to. And, for goodness sake, don't believe any old man who tells you that you'll get unlimited ice cream if you can eat them all without stopping. You'll get sick of them *and* you'll be the one who has to foot the bill.

Questions to Ask Yourself:

1. At what point is my work effort no longer productive? Do I find myself reading emails and scrolling pages without a sense of purpose?

2. When do I notice myself feeling stressed physically or emotionally about work? What strategies can I implement to reduce the stress levels and energize myself?

3. Have I ever been burned out before? Did I end up hating my work? Do I recognize the stressful situation that *caused* me to hate or resent my work/colleagues?

4. Have I quit a job or contemplated quitting a job because of the intensity of stress? What happened to my productivity before, during, and after those moments? What patterns do I notice?

5. Do I include breaks and rest as a part of my performance strategy? What can I do to assure that this happens?

Recognize Stress Signals and Manage Them

You are a problem solver. In every area of life, you're constantly solving problems.

No matter how good you are at it, it's impossible to operate in beast mode without having to eventually chill out and recharge the batteries. Daylight Savings Time, for some strange reason, is one of those reminders to relax… or else.

A study performed by the University of Colorado[2] showed that incidences of heart attacks have been reported to increase by 24% on the Monday following Daylight Savings Time.

Essentially, the thought of going back to work on Monday is already stressful enough and the thought of interrupting our sleep cycles makes the stress more than the heart can handle.

Fortunately, you don't need to wait for a heart attack to start thinking about managing stress. Stress management is a huge part of my work as a coach because everyone experiences stress and stress certainly doesn't discriminate on who it kills.

---

[2] https://openheart.bmj.com/content/1/1/e000019

What Are Stress Signals?

Stress signals are behaviors, moods, and physical symptoms that appear in a vast variety of forms.

From the classic headache, sleepless nights, and undesirable moods to relying on illicit drugs or medication, feeling constantly distracted, and engaging in destructive behaviors, stress signals can manifest at any level of stress.

Stress signals are often a consequence of consistent behaviors or emotional experiences that negatively affect performance and remind you that something has to change. *Now.*

I give clients a list of common stress signals to see if they identify with any of them. I do this because sometimes my clients don't even realize that they're experiencing a stress signal because they've learned to ignore their feelings.

Acknowledging and dealing with stress signals is sometimes the first thing I help clients deal with on the path of facing larger workplace issues because it's amazing how feeling relieved and relaxed can change our entire perspective on problems.

Stress signals say, "Hey, something is causing this stress and it's telling me about this situation. I need to do something differently to move forward in a better way."

Stress Signal Scenario

David is stressed and he knows it, but he's not clear on why. He gets frequent headaches and he feels out of sorts physically. He's also anxious about his work situation because conditions are constantly changing.

After some coaching, David realized that because he's so worried about getting fired, he's coping by taking his work home on the weekends, lying awake at night replaying the conflicts he's had with his colleagues, and he's stopped surfing because he just doesn't feel motivated to paddle out. The lack of sleep, exercise, and dependence on caffeine to stay awake are triggering his headaches and reveal the general lack of mental and physical balance he's experiencing. David's stress signals reveal a deep inner conflict.

Because David knows he can't just stroll into work and tell his colleagues they're all incompetent boneheads who are vastly under qualified for their jobs, he knows he's got to change his *own* habits in order to overcome the uncertainty at work and stop the vicious cycle that's wreaking havoc on his health and his morale.

Questions to Ask Yourself:

1. What are my stress signals (the signs that say something is not right)?
2. What are the behaviors or situations that are causing the stress signal?
3. What is the stress signal telling me about my situation or myself?
4. What has got to stop or change around me? Long term/short term?

What Are Energizers?

You don't have to be a Trekkie to be energized. Energizers are activities that increase energy, renew the spirit, and eliminate inner conflict. Personal to each of us, energizers are the choices that increase positive moods and help to resolve stressful work and life situations instead of ignoring them.

Energizers can be as small as going for an afternoon board session, meeting a friend for a cold brew, talking with a yoda-like friend, or chilling with family. Energizers can also be big things that take more time like driving along the coast, going on an epic vacation, or trying a new hobby. Energizers can even include meditating or simply doing nothing. Energizers help us to get perspective and shift moods.

Energizers say, "Ok, I know that I'm not feeling optimal right now… how can I step back and regroup, re-center, and relax?"

Energizer Scenario:

David acknowledges in coaching sessions that his work situation is tough and his colleagues aren't making things any easier. He knows his present behaviors aren't going to change things, either.

Before David can actually constructively deal with his work issues, he needs to feel better now. So, instead of drinking six espressos a day, he's down to two and is drinking water whenever he feels tired or thirsty. He sets up date nights with his wife to reconnect with her. He sets up an hour once every month with his mentor to get some perspective and he takes his kids surfing on Saturday mornings to get some laughs. While dealing with his stress signals head on, David's taking care of other areas of his life at the same time. Win-win.

Questions to Ask Yourself:

1. What activities give me energy, peace of mind, or motivate me?
2. How can I fit my energizers into my day, week, month?
3. Do my energizers help me constructively deal with, instead of ignoring, what is causing my stress? If not, what energizers can help me do that?

4. When I immediately sense stress creeping up on me, what can I immediately do to step back and relax? Who can I count on to help me if I need help?

Putting Stress Signals and Energizers to Work

Individuals who properly identify their stress signals and use their energizers can transform stress to their benefit, instead of their detriment.

Because David recognized his stress signals and employed his energizers, he then felt emotionally and physically prepared to handle his work issues: he's got more patience to respond to mind-numbing e-mails, he started improving his management skills, and he's got more clarity to come up with creative solutions to his larger workplace problems. He's on a brighter, more confident path.

Most stress signals aren't the end of the world (deadly heart attacks aside). Stress signals are cues for starting fresh and taking control of what we've allowed to temporarily control us. Once we've gotten re-energized, we're ready to get back into the game with a fresh attitude.

Work with Your Rhythms Instead of Against Them

Mornings begin by either finishing what you've started or starting something new.

Life is the constant process of beginnings and endings.

Mornings are usually purposeful. But, by the end of the day a general countdown vibe until final wind down begins.

What about those long hours between meal break and the hour before closing time? These are the hazy mental hours of the work day. How do we make the most of them?

Many of us get groggy and disoriented after lunch. After hunger has been satisfied and the most urgent matters have been addressed, the lull that happens next demands extra self-determination and priority management skills. This is the time when magic happens.

Come along with me for a while and entertain this concept….

This time between 1:00 PM and 4:00 PM is a great time to maintain what's been happening and follow up on what's been left hanging.

These are the tasks and conversations that require touching base and supervision. They don't require much mental concentration, nor physical force. So, you can work *with* the fatigue and drowsiness that follows lunch until you've garnered enough wind for a second round of concentration before quitting time.

These tasks can include reordering office supplies, putting water into the cooler, and dropping off the mail. If it's a regular thing you do that doesn't require too much mental focus, get up, physically move, and do it. Harnessing the power of gentle physical movement gets your digestive system flowing and gets your mind to follow the awareness of your body's rhythm.

Essentially, if you can't be mentally productive, at least get up and make yourself physically productive. Clean up, do dishes, replace the yogurt that belongs to your colleague that you "borrowed" from the fridge, file away and throw out piled up papers and deliver some mail.

Work through the brain fog, not in spite of it.

If you can't even recognize an opportunity to help out and catch up on chores ask yourself, "What have I been wanting to do that I have not had dedicated time to do?"

Use this time to explore and honor yourself.

Google calls it the **70/20/10**[3] ratio. Use a couple of hours to explore new concepts and opportunities that may have absolutely nothing to do with your work and whatever strikes your fancy. If you're going to waste the time walking in circles, playing around on Pinterest, or taking a nap in a bathroom stall, you might as well explore something totally off the wall. You might just have some fun *and* come up with an amazing insight or solution.

Once you start to perk up and regain some energy and mental focus, switch gears and wrap up work that needs

---

[3] https://en.wikipedia.org/wiki/70/20/10_Model

finishing. You'll thank yourself for committing to your responsibilities, getting things done, and giving yourself time to explore the realm of possibilities with no consequences. By the end of the day, you'll have made the most of every moment and will have lots to show.

Allow yourself to *go with the flow* instead of pushing against it and stopping it!

Each of us has a natural body and concentration rhythm. When it comes to performance, work with your own rhythms by gaining awareness of what comes naturally, what patterns exist, and what regularly needs maintenance.

This "hazy" time is an opportunity to work harmoniously *with yourself* instead of forcing yourself to go through the motions.

You'll be surprised how much more enjoyable, relaxing, and productive this time can really be.

Questions to Ask Yourself:

1. Do I try to force myself to be productive? Do I feel guilty when I'm not getting something done?
2. Would it be OK if I accepted my natural rhythm and worked in harmony with myself instead of trying to work by arbitrary deadlines?
3. Do I know how to manage my energy in relation to my schedule? Am I setting realistic goals, rather than unrealistic expectations?
4. Am I judging myself harshly for not completing goals by a specific time or date?
5. Do I compare my progress to other's progress?

6. How can I start taking better care of myself while I fulfill my duties and dreams each day?
7. Do I know when to say, "I've done enough, today"?

Be a Leader Instead of Manager

Leadership is akin to taking a group through a great desert, not totally knowing what lies ahead.

Leadership is guiding people, especially ourselves, into an uncharted wilderness.

Those who want to know what to expect out of their actions are managers. This, too, is perfectly O.K.. There is, however, nothing visionary about achieving something that's already been done and expected. Leaders know this and are willing to take on the challenge of making real what presently exists in the imagination.

Leaders are those who sometimes find themselves awake at night with the sobering realization that, despite having a vision, they really don't know how things will work out to make it real.

Leaders don't totally know how the fulfillment of their vision will come about. Leaders don't always know how the means of fulfillment will come about. And, what unknown territories actually mean within the span of their careers. But, leaders have got an inkling, an intangible feeling that propels them forward.

An unseen pull to progress and to go beyond all the other experiences that you've experienced exists within you.

As a leadership coach, I can tell a leader from a manager from a mile away. One wants to push forward, prepared to abandon all their preconceived notions as to what success feels and looks like. While the manager clings to maintain more of the same, sometimes preferring yesterday to today.

Anyone who insists that they just want to go back to what they were doing before isn't ready to move forward, let alone lead others forward.

I get it. Change can be hard.

Sometimes, change feels painful, confusing, and just damned hard.

And yet, the individual who is ready to accept change is ready to accept the opportunity of entering into that vision.

Individuals who detach themselves from *how* things *should* be are mentally open enough to *deal* with circumstances as they *are*. And are thus prepared to *adapt to* change.

The thing is, anyone who has been working long enough knows that the business environment is constantly changing. It's not like you have to force things to evolve. Change is the only constant.

Thus, an adaptive leader understands this fact and is willing to confront changing conditions and work in harmony with them - even those unexpected and tough changes. Adaptive leaders see the opportunities left open by the changing tides and go for them.

Granted, conditions may not always be ideal. And so, leaders who possess enough fortitude to keep going ultimately learn from the indices that the environment is communicating and can thus choose their next best action.

Like walking through an uncharted desert, we don't always know what awaits us on the road ahead - and that can feel daunting.

Leaders, while having a vision in mind, are not attached to ways and means of fulfillment. Rather, leaders embrace the challenges and conditions of the uncharted territory in which they are leading their team and can realize their dreams with every step forward.

Leading isn't always a fearless activity. It's one in which we must embrace the fear and go forward anyway. This attitude is what defines a courageous leader.

Embracing the unknown is a healthy exercise in leadership development because the act says, "I don't need the past, nor the future to define me. I just need what resources I've got in me to give me the tools so I can use them to be better and do better."

Questions to Ask Yourself:

1. Do I cling to the past? My past successes, failures, unresolved issues? Do I live my career and thus my expectations, too much into the future?

2. When "going through the desert" do I pay attention to the conditions around me and allow them to communicate to me where there are the opportunities for improvement?

3. What are my fears? What are they saying to me? How are they trying to help and, at the same time, holding me back?

4. When I lead people, do I get them to focus on growth experiences instead of punishing them for missteps? Do I give myself the same grace?

5. Do I just want to maintain what's happening by resisting change or do I allow myself to go with the flow of change? Which scenario best describes me? Why/why not?

6. When it comes to the strategy of achieving what it is that I want, do I go the paths that have already been traversed or do I allow myself to walk my own path? Where does the conflict within myself lie?

ATTITUDE

Get Your Inner Team in Sync

The conscious mind has an agenda - to stay safe - to not rock the boat, to float along the tides of history, so that we don't go overboard. The conscious mind has bills to pay, a reputation to protect, and people to answer to. This part of us is domesticated like cattle in a herd.

There is another part of us that challenges known safety and wants to take risks, jump off the ledge, and cannot be tamed. It does what it wants and does the job for another part that needs to grow in order to fully realize itself.

You have three parts of your self that are sometimes at conflict:

1. The part that has to grow and evolve: your spirit, your power and presence.
2. The rebel adventurer who blazes trails and makes a way: your will; habits and impulses.
3. The part that wants to fit in and survive so that our spirit and will can keep doing what they're doing: your mind; the decision maker.

Often, we find ourselves in conflict with these parts. It's like organizing the troops, or better yet, getting a pen of puppies to sit still.

With this conflict in mind, ask yourself an important question:

How do you get your mind to call the shots in a way to channel your will to do its job effectively so that your spirit's needs are met?

The mind is the boss of the will in a way that it tells it what to do and the will gets to work.

"Ha!" we laugh, "*Try telling that to a lifelong smoker.*"

The mind will say, *"I really need to quit smoking."* But the hand picks up the cigarette anyway.

Discipline is consciously commanding your will to do something and actually following through.

How many times have we said, "I'll get up super early to surf," and actually slept in instead?

There's something that your will needs more than what your conscious mind thinks it needs. It's trying to help your spirit to break through the confines of your mind.

Take a person who wants to find a full time job in a company instead of the freelance business that they have. They're doing everything they can to apply for jobs, networking, asking around, applying on Malakye, etc. But nothing is landing and this person becomes resentful towards the system. What their conscious mind hasn't yet realized is that their freelance schedule (even if it doesn't pay all the bills) makes this person available for their family, so they can help out at a moment's notice; something a full time job would not likely permit them to do.

So, to help get the spirit, will, and mind working together, the mind would have to understand what the spirit is doing. The will and the mind need to make peace with the fears regarding the family issues. This process would then help the mind to break free of the self-limiting behaviors and help grow the spirit so the fears are no longer an issue.

I know what I'm saying sounds like a bunch of psychobabble, but try it and see for yourself. Observe the conflict between the parts of your inner team and notice how resolving the inner conflict impacts your relationships with larger groups, like teams and organizations.

How aware of your self-discipline are you?
Are you in alignment or are you working against yourself?

A house divided cannot stand. Trust your inner adventurer, listen to what your spirit needs, and make choices that will help you realize your own version of heaven on earth. You'll be surprised as to how effective your inner team can really be.

Questions to Ask Yourself:

1. When I think about my career intentions, do I get caught up in all the things I'll have to do and deal with in the future? Or, do I focus on what I can do now?

2. Am I a time traveler? Meaning, do I spend my time anticipating problems in the possible timelines of achieving my goals? If so, how can I get grounded in the present?

3. Do I doubt my abilities and knowledge when I think about my potential? What kind of negative self-talk do I engage myself in? What are a few positive things I can say about my potential?

4. Am I committed to being the very best professional and person I can be right now? Will I give myself the dedication, self-love, and in-sight necessary to achieve growth?

5. When I work on my goals, do I look towards where I'm going or do I allow myself to get distracted? What kind of procrastination do I engage in?

The Secret to Making Lasting First Impressions

When meeting people for the first time in the business world, there is a tendency to think more about what people want from us or what we can get from other people. People forget the simple honor of being welcomed into someone else's mental, emotional, and physical space.

And, the excitement of meeting someone and all of the possibilities (positive and negative) associated with that meeting can be intimidating to ponder. Anticipatory anxiety makes business meetings and interviews all the more nerve wracking.

When making first impressions, we worry a lot about what we're going to say:

Will I say something dumb?
Will I say something I'll regret?
Will I put my big, fat foot in my mouth?

Goodness, I have felt that way before meeting a client for the first time.

I wondered, "*Can I help this person? What if I make a mistake?*"

Meeting people for the first time is a humbling experience to say the least.

Nevertheless, I am constantly reminded time and time again that meeting someone for the first time isn't focused on what we have to say as much as how well we listen to the subtle messages that we're hearing throughout our initial conversation. And, through the act of listening, connections are effortlessly forged instead of uselessly forced.

Simply being interested makes you interesting.

Have you ever met someone who goes on and on about themselves? I can hear groans as I write this. It's because, contrary to their belief, these people are not giving to us, but they're sucking our energies dry. Working with someone who is self-absorbed is dreadful. Which is why I encourage my clients to worry less about what they have to say about themselves during interviews and focus more on asking questions directed at bridging the gap between themselves and potential employers or partners. Through this process, our best interview answers come out and shine.

In other words, I ask you to consider:

How will you give the right interview answers and make the right impression if you don't care to ask for more information that can shape and give direction to your answer?

When we know more, we are more empowered to share our unique and authentic responses that can reveal our truest self and our very best qualities.

Dale Carnegie said that the fastest way to make friends and influence people is to care about others and their interests, "The royal road to a man's heart is to talk to him about the things he treasures most."

Sure, people can be vain and insipid creatures. I'm not recommending feigning interest or sucking up to people in order to make the best first impression. Rather, I recommend you get out of your own head and set your ego aside to sincerely take a deeper look at those with whom you've been given the honor to meet. It's through people and our relationships with them that reveal the most about ourselves and the impressions we give and receive.

You don't have to sit around a circle smoking a peace pipe to make a great first impression, but you can offer your interest, sincerity, and authenticity to everyone we meet so as to leave a lasting, positive impression.

Questions to Ask Yourself:

1. What is a more important priority when meeting people for the first time: Telling people about myself or learning about their needs and interests? How can I shift my focus?

2. When I worry about the first impression I'll make, can I come up with a few creative and simple ice breaker questions to open up the exchange?

3. When interviewers tell me about the open position's job related issues, should I focus on how the problems affect me or how I can positively contribute to the solution?

4. When thinking about the possibilities of meeting someone for the first time, do I automatically jump to conclusions about how the relationship will pan out? What questions can I ask to gain a better understanding instead of jumping to conclusions about the people I meet?

Developing and Mastering Fluency in Nonverbal Communication

Body language is more than simply attracting the opposite sex. After all, there is more to life and social interactions than doing the nasty.

What if I told you that there is more to body language than meets the eye?

What if you are attracting and repelling career and business opportunities without even knowing it?

That, with a flick of a wrist, a sigh, a turn of the head, or an eye roll you're speaking a language in which you are very fluent?

Those who can read and master their own body language are comfortable within themselves and their environment. There's an unconscious competence to speaking body language and those who speak it fluently are creatively powerful.

Intriguing, yes?

There is a lot to learn by reading body language. People tell us more through mere movement and sound than through the words they express. After all, a vast majority of communication is nonverbal. Going into a boardroom and watching board members and executives is like watching a game of poker: everyone around the table has their tells for displeasure, excitement, happiness, boredom and more. There is so much posturing, one would swear the room was full of peacocks.

Disengaging Conflict: Matching and Refocusing
Reading body language can not only engage you with audiences, but it can help you detach from drama that could otherwise suck you into unnecessary work and emotional frenzy. Without words, you are being told when someone isn't in the mood to talk or if they want to vent their frustrations.

By looking carefully at the signs of unhappiness and displeasure, you can disengage by simply choosing not to mirror their behavior. If someone makes an unhappy face, instead make a happy face. If they make an unhappy sound, instead make a happy sound. Physical incongruence keeps drama from building.

Now, if you've been sucked in already, what can you do?

Someone is pissed off and you realize that you've gone too far and things can go even more disastrously. This is the opportunity to meet them where they are at now, at their tone and level of intensity, and then start taking things down a notch. If someone is worked up, match their vocal level and feelings of intensity. Want to piss them off even more? Get louder or more physically expressive and see what happens (at your own risk).

For example, if someone says, "Damn, I can't believe I have to deal with this problem again! Why does this constantly happen?!"

You could respond with an equally frustrated voice and then taper off into a more inquisitive and gentle tone, "I know! This sucks! It feels like you've been dealt a crappy hand! Although, I wonder if there are some solutions so that, imagine now, things didn't have to keep ending up this way?"

Meeting someone where they are at *first* allows the person to know that we're on the same page and then allows you their permission to take their frustration level down a notch by refocusing their attention to a solution oriented mindset *after*.

Muscle Memory: Carrying Old Physical Behaviors into New Territory

You have been using your old body language vocabulary through unconscious conditioning (think Pavlov's dogs) that you don't even realize you're taking your old patterns and applying them to totally new and different situations - and that doesn't always serve you. Ever heard of the phrase *muscle memory?*

Albert Einstein said that we can't solve new problems with old ways of thinking, which is why it's important to be ever mindful of your body language when meeting new people in new contexts. New people tell us through their own physical cues what to look out for and how they learn and communicate within the framework of their minds. Which means they're practically handing us a wide open opportunity to join them in their world. And what do you do? You ignore the signs and go on living in your own world.

Pay attention to how someone moves and the sounds they make upon meeting them for the first time. Now, pay attention to yours. What does your body language say? Your body language and vocal patterns are often so embedded with old memories (positive and negative) and that you're unconsciously reliving old experiences with the same physical patterns. You're taking your unconscious muscle memory into new experiences, thus repeating old patterns.

The goal of fluently speaking body language is to become unconsciously competent of reading other people's body language so that you can match and lead them instinctively. Can you do this? If not, read on.

Developing Fluency: Reading Body Language

You don't have to spend years studying the art of body language, neuro linguistic programming, or even cognitive behavioral psychology to read and interpret body language.

You just need to keep your eyes and ears open to the subtle signals people send you - like little ham radios, it's possible to naturally and instinctively pick up signals and moreover *understand* them.

Practice.

Practice by taking a look at loved ones: friends, lovers, children and reading their signals.

What are they saying?

What are their tells?

How can you tell your lover or child is lying?

How can you tell that they're hiding something?

When they're happy?

Pay close attention to these cues and then go into work and watch colleagues closely in a meeting.

Imagine first, as if the sound of the conversation was completely taken out. Just watch what's going on - look at the faces, the hands, feet and other extremities - and try to read the nuances of the situation just by these cues alone.

What can you deduce from simple physical cues?

Now, try pretending to be blind and listen carefully to vocal intonations. Does someone say something they should be confident about, but finish the sentence in the form of a question? Pay attention to the incongruencies of what a person is saying versus the simultaneous sound or physical motion that accompanies it.

The simple practice of reading physical cues and sounds and asking questions to explore these signals are all it takes to become better fluent in "body language." Receptivity grows by first being consciously incompetent and through practice a natural unconscious competence forms.

Speaking Body Language: Being Subtly Influential

By understanding body language and speaking it (by matching or by being incongruent) fluently, it's delightfully surprising to see how relationships build and projects move forward easily and creatively.

Matching body language makes us more attractive (because people see themselves unconsciously in us) and makes deflecting negative attitudes more graceful (by choosing not to match their body language). This means, quite simply, that you now have the power to experience what you want and release what you don't need.

Don't believe me? Challenge yourself to move and use vocal intonations that you don't normally use and begin to experience the subtle dynamic shifts with the people you encounter. By controlling your own body language in response to the situations you find yourself in, you can take back your own power and actively give yourself choices instead of waiting for them to be given to you.

A final thought: *Let your language be love and speak it so fluently that any other language is indecipherable.*

Questions to Ask Yourself:

1. Think back to when you or someone else de-escalated a dramatic situation? What physical things did they do? How did they sound? How did the dramatic/upset person react?

2. Think about your own body language reading skills for a moment. When meeting new people, do you watch how they move and adjust your physical and vocal intonations accordingly? Can you tell when they are incongruent to your own body movement?

3. What is your common body language "vocabulary"? Do you say the same "words" over and over again? Can you challenge yourself to act/sound differently?

4. When was the last time you noticed a person's body language? How did their body language reveal about their feelings/moods?

5. Think about someone you want to avoid. How do you physically move or sound? Now, think about someone you want to attract. How do you act? Now, think about situations in which you are indifferent. How do you act compared to when you are trying to attract something? What are the subtle differences?

Embracing Small Victories

What makes a big success?
What's the difference between large and small victories?
And, is success an attitude or is it a process?
Find out now...
Achievement is often equated to a singular event in which something good and substantial occurs. When these *important* events happen, you feel elated and in tune with the world around you. When they don't, especially when you expect *what* that big thing is and *when* it should happen, you can be left feeling angry, resentful, and confused. There is a sense of alienation that creeps in. That is, when you believe you've been cut off from your desired results, you believe that you must be on the wrong path.

At what point do you consider yourself a winner?
When the victory has already passed?
When the moment of achievement is at the peak of the moment? Or before the event has even occurred?
Professional athletes do what is often called visualization. They imagine themselves performing before they're even on the field. They imagine in their minds each successful twist and turn

that leads up to and creates in its totality the achievement of which they imagine themselves having attained. With that said, achievement isn't only a result - achievement is a process.

Processes are a series of steps taken in order to achieve a result or end.

I know, I know - I hear you saying and have heard you say in person at The Shmooz, *"But I've done everything right and I still don't get the results I want."*

Let's ask some honest questions here: Have you really done *everything* "right"? And, why are you disappointed that the process you went through gave you the results you currently experience?

You succeeded in getting an undesired result. In other words, you got so caught up on the results and the big victories that you disconnected the fully manifested result from the cumulative process.

When this disconnect happens, we overlook the importance of the processes. The process is the steps, the attitudes, and the small victories that are actually the achievement in and of itself. Disconnect is when we try to take short cuts, cut corners, ignore our needs and the needs of others, and try to win big at all costs.

Take the analogy of a redwood tree in all its gigantic glory. At what point does one decide when a redwood tree is impressive and beautiful? Was it when it was a seed? Or, when it made its way through the soil or when it surpassed trees of normal height? Or, when it finally reached its maximum height? Some amongst us might even be disappointed that the giant redwood didn't get as big as expected - maybe by a few meters.

The aforementioned questions are aimed to ask you something important: **At what point do you decide that you're successful and victorious?**

What if professional success isn't one giant moment in which everything "magically" aligns and when everyone else recognizes you?

What if, instead, success is in being, not in finishing?

I hear many coaching clients tell me, *"I'll be happy when..."* and *"When I see that result, then I'll turn around my attitude."*

Delaying the habitual feeling of success forever places rewards into the future. So, why not now?

I've heard other clients say, *"It's cool that this (event) happened... but I still can't make ends meet... what's in it for me."*

These individuals can't mindfully acknowledge, let alone be grateful for, the fact that something good has just happened for them. They rather focus on what is lacking instead of being grateful for the small victory that they just experienced.

What good does it serve to work with professionals who can't notice success of all kinds - even if it hits them in the face?

Small victories are opportunities for more success. If you can't be in the frame of mind to *recognize* success, then how can you possibly *be* one?

Successful companies are process oriented, seeing success is attainable in every step, not just in the big payoff. And, successful professionals want to work with other people who recognize success in every form (big and small). Because success is both an attitude and an eternal process of learning and opportunity.

To answer the questions about the redwoods - what if the redwood was glorious at every stage? The redwood doesn't say to itself - *I'll be happy when I've reached 380 feet.* It honors itself where it is in its growth stage, not just in its maturity.

Questions to Ask Yourself:

1. Do you tend to focus on the end game rather than the process?

2. Do you get anxious about the future? Do you feel inadequate and won't feel good about yourself until you've reached a certain point?

3. Do you feel unsatisfied with yourself? What do you feel unsatisfied with?

4. Can you allow yourself to enjoy where you are at right now? What have you experienced recently that filled you with satisfaction?

Why Career Disasters Are Teachable Moments

We all hit speed bumps on the road of success.

These speed bumps can be translated to mean blunders and other disasters. You don't have to see speed bumps as destructive and costly. Rather, they can be golden opportunities that reveal new skills and higher understanding about your attitudes and actions that slowed you down in the first place.

I don't know anybody, including myself, that hasn't experienced a humbling moment in which we've made an ignorant or arrogant mistake. I got so caught up in the fast pace of work that I began to speed wobble, hit a bump, and face planted into my own mess. Leveled to the ground and picking the gravel of my failures out of my thin skin, it was hard to pick myself up and actually get back into the groove.

Getting caught up in and prolonging that moment of licking wounds costs more time and opportunity than actually dusting off and fixing the problem. Here's why:

Look Around: Slow Down For a Teachable Moment

Career disasters and other lesser mistakes can be thought of as speed bumps.

Speed bumps are put out for our own safety.

Speed bumps show there are other things around that are worth slowing down and taking a careful look at. And, in this case, to take a moment to examine behaviors and attitudes that led up to mistakes. Speed bumps are beneficial for the journey because great learning opportunities could be missed.

Professor and physicist Robert J. Havighurst popularized this kind of thinking with the term "teachable moments."[4] Teachable moments involve learning a developmental skill at the right moment making task achievement possible. Professional mistakes are opportunities to make things right. And we can. The question is *How*?

Recognizing a learning opportunity is the moment to make things right and correct the trajectory. Slowing things down provides a chance to identify areas of weaknesses and transform them into strengths.

From these situations two choices present themselves: A) sulk about the disaster and point fingers as to who did us wrong and remove any sense of personal responsibility about the crisis or B) look within for responsibility and insight and apply it into the situation in order to correct the course. Fortunately, most people choose option B and with good reason: *it pays off*.

Instant Decisions: Taking Responsibility For the Sake of the Future

While licking wounds, it's possible to instantly decide to walk off the pain or sulk in it. Depending on the choice, that instantaneous decision can either jump start you or weigh you down.

---

[4] https://en.wikipedia.org/wiki/Teachable_moment

It's not necessary to have a game plan right away. The simple act of reaching out and deciding that something, *anything* can be different and by goodness, better, is critical. In my experience of coaching pros who have made what appears to be some kind of irrevocable mistake, this powerful moment of taking responsibility for change can alone inspire creativity that seemingly comes out of nowhere.

Taking this giant leap into owning up to mistakes and contributions to the disasters we co-create is just the first step of mitigating their residual effects. Mistakes are errors in judgment. If left to fester, mistakes grow into unwanted circumstances that infect other areas of relationships, self-image, and lost business opportunities (in layman's terms: nobody wants to work with a jerk and if they can help it, certainly *not again*). Reaching out to those that we've hurt or seriously inconvenienced to take the first big step of owning up to our attitudes and behaviors is a part of that process of making things right and moving things forward in a positive direction.

Adversities Are Golden Opportunities in Disguise

Having slowed down during a teachable moment in addition to having taken ownership of and communicated your missteps, you are now free to transform a calamity into a golden opportunity.

Adversities are golden opportunities in disguise.

Golden opportunities allow you to remember the values you stand for and what you may have forgotten in the demand of work.

Through golden opportunities you can choose to say now, *"I've forgotten some of my core values and those we share and because of that we're here now. I can't change the past, but together, you and I can certainly change the outcome of this situation now."*

Disasters can be confusing times, but they don't have to snowball into even more stressful situations. So, the next time you find yourself in a mess, instead of instinctively developing a faster speed, slow down, own the moment, and focus on building a brighter path ahead. A path paved in gold. Golden opportunities, that is.

Questions to Ask Yourself:

1. When reflecting on a career disaster, what were the signals that warned me to slow down and reconsider my actions?

2. What were the key behaviors or attitudes that negatively influenced this present situation? How can I change or eliminate them for the future?

3. Where can I take ownership in this situation? Who needs to hear this in order to move forward?

4. Realizing that I've been gifted the golden opportunity of a teachable moment, what can I learn in order to overcome adversity?

How Gratitude Puts You in Charge

Gratitude is a feeling that flows and permeates in all aspects of life, because it's a choice; a choice to see, feel, and experience the opportunity in the world around us. Gratitude is an act of taking stock of the good available to us.

Respond or React: Choosing Our Paradigms to Influence the World

We've all experienced moments in our lives and careers in which there seemed very little to be thankful for: overbearing bosses, trying economic environments, wasted talent, conflict, and the general discomfort of life experiences.

Take a moment to think about these types of experiences and feel the discomfort in your body. It's easy to go to a place where anger, helplessness, and hopelessness live.

Now, going to a place, a place where it seems that you have to put effort into actually thinking about (and taking into account) all of the things you have to be grateful for, feel and experience from this point of view.

From both places, what you have left is choice.

The question is: What *kind of choices do these paradigms offer me?*

And from here, what choices will you select to best respond? Because, after all, your choices reflect how you see yourself - not the situations unfolding around you. For, reaction is simply doing what was done to you by doing the same. Response, however, is answering the problem; not giving back the same thought (or thoughtlessness) from where the problem came.

Hidden Wisdom: Gratitude Gives Opportunities to Exercise More Choice

Gratitude is the choice to see the problems around us as opportunities to exercise *more* choice.

Clients come to me with problems and they're often angry. They just want to get rid of their problems, stop them, and get past them. Fair enough.

As a coach, I see opportunity and hidden wisdom within the problems.

Whether through coaching or hypnosis, I ask, *"What is the wisdom to be gained from a self-sabotaging behavior or an unwanted situation?"*

Consciously, one might not be aware of that wisdom. But given time to reflect and go deeper, problems and struggles reveal a hidden wisdom that is trying to come to the surface.

Once acknowledged and thanked, the newly integrated wisdom seems to transform personal and professional difficulties into opportunities to act on. Thereby, providing more opportunities to make a choice.

Accounting & Accountability: Gratitude Takes Back Your Power To Choose

Reflecting on the Charlie Hebdo tragedy in France, as a French citizen I was initially angry and sad. For two days, I mourned the loss of my people, the youth, and the life gone.

At first, I wanted to get to the bottom of things and finger who to blame. But then, the questions came to me... *And then what? What would I do then? What about my own accountability?* What about *my* choices *now?* Whoa. The tragedy put the spotlight back on me, my choices, and my paradigm of France, the world, and ultimately my own power.

Suddenly, I had a lot to be grateful for, to recognize, and take into account. The attitude of gratitude once again reminded me of my ability to choose... and to choose differently from the perpetrators. Maybe, the individuals involved in the terrorist attack believed they didn't have choice, power, and much to be grateful for... Maybe, their sense of power came from exercising a choice - maybe the only choice they believed they had. But, at the end of the day, these are stories people create to take the responsibility and power out of their own hands to justify the behaviors and situations they believe are not of their choosing. The truth is, you have a choice even when you believe you don't.

Gratitude, on the other hand, takes power, choice, and potential for change and puts everything back into your own hands. Gratitude is the act of recognizing your power to choose, to select from the inventory of resources and wisdom available to you, and gives you a platform to act in accord with your authentic self.

When you enjoy the company of your colleagues, friends, and family (and even perfect strangers), reflect upon the power of choice. Take stock of what your choices have provided you (maybe freedom, abundance, love, fulfillment) and recognize the direct influence you have on the world around you. Just knowing these facts gives you a lot to be grateful for.

Questions to Ask Yourself:

1. When looking at a chain of choices that I have made, what have these choices given me? What do they tell me about myself, my beliefs, and my behaviors?

2. What stories do I create that take my power to choose out of my hands? What situations and self-sabotaging behaviors keep cropping up that make me feel powerless?

3. When I am faced with difficult situations, do I choose to look at them from a cynical point of view? What choices do I give myself when I do so?

4. When I make choices, are they out of reaction (feeding back what I got) or responding (giving a solution to a problem)? Why?

5. Do I actively take into account my accountability and what resources I have to make a direct impact on the situations around me? Why/why not? How can I hold myself more accountable?

Get Off the Grid and Reconnect with Yourself

Going off the grid.

It can mean anything to anybody. But *really*, what does getting off the grid really mean?

Does getting off the grid imply some negative image? That, somehow, implies total isolation and disconnection from everyone and everything? Believe it or not, "getting off the grid" can mean something else entirely, and can, in effect, make more meaningful and clearer connections with the world around us possible.

For the longest time, when someone said the phrase "getting off the grid" I had this image of an old man, living in the mountains, salty as all get go, and paranoid about the government getting ahold of his private information in some grand conspiracy theory.

There are more relaxing and wholesome ways to get off the grid. The benefits of getting off the grid, even for only a day, are astounding. Disconnecting permits building stronger connections.

After feeling that initial sense of overwhelm ask yourself, "Why do I need to get off the grid in the first place?"

Usually, when we need to disconnect, it's because there is a strong overwhelm of information that isn't being channeled or processed. This could be because of burnout from work (too much work, not enough rest or energizers), too much information and not enough quiet time to process it all, or stressful situations that happen back to back without much downtime to get a fresh perspective. These are just a few signs indicating why it's important to disconnect and get off the grid for a while. It's not enough, however, to know that the need is real, but to also understand why we have to do so.

Getting off the grid is an opportunity to step back and nurture ourselves.

Take a moment and imagine a time and place where you pulled all your energy back and recentered yourself. That's what getting off the grid is: It's disconnecting our emotional, mental, and physical focus and bringing it back to us in order to reconnect with ourselves.

Ever heard someone say, "Awe, man, I'm just all over the place!"

This is one of those catchphrases signaling that it's time to get off the grid and reconnect with ourselves. And, fortunately, there are so many ways (besides disconnecting from our mobile devices) that'll help us do just that.

That overwhelmed feeling that you're all over the place and disjointed makes for the perfect situational asset that can teach you about your behaviors and choices at work and in life.

It says, "Let's reverse engineer this situation in order to figure out why and how we've got here."

Because, let's face it, our mobile devices aren't glued to our hands. There's an underlying reason why we feel addicted to looking at it all of the time. And while cutting the habit of constantly looking at emails or Instagram cold turkey may temporarily stop that behavior, it certainly won't eliminate the feeling that started it in the first place.

Getting off the grid is the perfect opportunity to examine unhealthy habits while in a restful and contemplative state.

Whether by surfing, camping in the wilderness, spending the summer in Europe, or just taking a few hours or a day to just get recentered - these are just a few of the perfect ways to reconnect with your most authentic and healthy self.

Getting off the grid certainly does not have to mean disconnecting from the world and forgoing your job, responsibilities, and loved ones while figuring yourself out. For most of us, our lives aren't like the book *Into The Wild*. My clients are people with families, full lives, and a network of people who rely on their commitments. Disconnecting for a little while permits a joyful return to their lives.

You truly know what is best for you. Getting a chance to reconnect with your own inner truth and wisdom by, even temporarily, disconnecting from distractions and overwhelming feelings provides clarity.

Getting off the grid affords an opportunity to listen to your still small voice. It'll tell you why you do the things you do, what you get out of whatever unhealthy behavior or old attitude you carry with you into new situations, and more importantly, what you can do about it.

Getting off the grid is a chance to be gentle with yourself without a harsh, critical eye. Give yourself a chance to find out what's best for you and to take that wisdom back into your everyday, vastly connected life. Having created a safe, non-critical mental environment it's the perfect space to come up with fresh insights for new ways of living and working.

So, by getting off the grid - shutting yourself off into a quiet place, turning off the boob-tube, or switching off the wifi, temporarily retreating somewhere - can actually be a healthy activity and way to create a sense of wholeness and personal well-being.

Essentially, getting off the grid doesn't have to mean becoming a salty anti-social hermit to avoid getting caught up in psychological dramas. Allow situations to indicate that it's time for you to pull back and look inside instead of outside of yourself. Cut off the outer noise and increase the pure sound of your own inner truth. Never know, you might just like what you hear.

Questions to Ask Yourself:

1. Do I get overwhelmed by events or conditions in my life? What events or circumstances overwhelm me the most?

2. Do I distract myself by looking at social media, the news, or programming to avoid dealing with my feelings?

3. Do I give myself moments in my day to be focused on my own energy and feelings? If not, when can I just be with myself without interruptions?

4. When was the last time that I got in touch with my motivations and emotions? What is motivating me right now? How do my emotions reflect my motivations?

5. Do I allow external events and conditions to tell me how I should feel? If so, what kinds of feelings are they giving me? If not, what feelings do I decide to feel on a regular basis?

PERSONAL BRANDING

Six Personal Brand Building Strategies

The phrase "personal branding" has been so overused that it hardly feels personal anymore.

Check out six ways to put the person back into personal branding to build more authentic relationships and a meaningful career.

1. Let It Go and Act Natural

Let go of whatever you think you should *be* or should *have*. Embrace what you presently have and allow who you really are to shine.

Acting naturally, believe it or not, is not very natural to many people.

A personal brand isn't about forcing things or relationships to happen, but instead letting your message appeal to the people or groups that understand you without having to overtly explain or justify yourself.

When this happens, career frustrations and blocks seem to fall away and your natural relationships will blossom on their own. When we're at most ease with ourselves, the doors to growth opportunities appear and open effortlessly.

2. You Can Do It - But You Can't Do Everything

As the old saying goes, *we can't make everyone happy.* That goes with your own positioning in the job market and what goes on your resume. There are a million jobs out there, but only one that's right for you.

What are your strengths?

What are the specific skills and knowledge areas that you have to offer? To whom?

You can't do everything, so specialization is the key to personal branding. By knowing what you're good at and where you shine, it's easier to tell your story and find places to fit in.

3. Building Trust Is Saying One Thing a Million Different Ways

A personal brand is based on trust. Trust creates a solid foundation that people can rely on when life is confusing or when the future seems unclear. Trust takes time to build through consistency and persistence. Trust is consistently saying the same thing in a million different ways.

In other words, let everything you do have the same fundamental message.

An excellent resume demonstrates a variety of different projects with the same general message of personal expression. Bosses, clients, and colleagues can count on you to help them through challenging times and they're more willing to go along with you in the face of change. Persistent consistency builds lasting trust.

4. Nurture Yourself and See What Grows

Building a personal brand takes work: **work on yourself**.

Building a brand around service to others doesn't mean giving ourselves until it hurts. It's a balancing act that helps us nurture ourselves, work on existing and developing new skills, and grow to be the best people and professionals possible. Working on yourself includes adjusting your paradigms about your work relationships, the kind of work you do and the value you create, and what kind of satisfaction you attain through your work.

By taking time to reflect - through breaks, vacation, and personal time - you afford yourself an opportunity to see your work with fresh eyes and a newfound sense of understanding that you can share.

5. Creating Positive Change Through a Personal Brand

A personal brand does not mean you have to be at an expert level.

You're having a human experience and sometimes experience errors in judgment.

Knowing your strengths comes out of the process of acknowledging failures of logic and choosing to make different choices. This process is called positive change and makes your story even more intriguing.

Overcoming personal and professional obstacles can be daunting, especially where there seems to be so much competition, but it can be done in small, workable steps. People love to hear success stories where people overcome their adversities.

If you don't like your current personal brand, you can change it - and as a result, how people see you. Once again, persistent consistency is the key to positive change.

6. Stay Focused and Know Thyself

With so many out there doing their own thing - some succeeding and others failing - it's possible to get distracted and try to copy others who seem to be more successful.

My advice is to avoid this mental trap. Your authentic voice can't get lost in the noise of distraction. Take stock of your strengths and get to know those who appreciate you for you and the specific skills sets and knowledge you have to share.

Know thyself is the best and most succinct advice on branding - know what works, what doesn't, when to dig in and stand your ground, and when to step back to regain perspective. By trusting your authentic self, people will see that and trust it, too.

Questions to Ask Yourself:

1. What are my strongest job skills, personality traits, and areas of expertise?
2. Who seems to appreciate me the most? Can I list any specific business associates, companies, or clients?
3. What are the things I *think* I should have or be in my career? What expectations do I hold about myself and my career? Do they help me or frustrate me?
4. When do I take the time to nurture myself? Do I take vacations or breaks to reflect on what I've accomplished and unwind the stress that has built up?
5. What does my personal brand say about me? Do others trust me? Why/why not?
6. What mistakes or failures have I made? What can I learn that can help me evolve my brand or help others?
7. What values do I know about myself as a professional to be true (and hope others see)?

How Do You Know When You're Successful?

Moments of reflection are great opportunities to create fresh starts and for re-analyzing goals and motivations. Pauses are a great way to analyze how you're using your time and directing your attention.

No matter what has happened in the past, a moment of reflection begs the question, "What's next in my career?"

Are you going to keep doing what you're doing? Are you going to create more of the same? Or, are you going to switch things up and enter into new experiences? It's totally up to you.

My clients have asked themselves these questions.

Some have said to me, "I want things to be totally different… but I don't care to change what I'm doing."

You have to take a minute to work through that train of thought.

People ask, "If change is inevitable, then can change just happen *for* me? Can change preferably not happen *to* me? Especially when it's 'bad' stuff?

It all depends on our mindset and what direction we've got it pointed in.

Likening this concept with the compass metaphor, take a moment to set your inner compass into the direction of your dreams.

What are your dreams? What do they look like? Can you be specific?

Can you dream up your goals with your imagination?

Most can quite easily. Everyone has the capacity to imagine how things can be different.

Feeling good about circumstances in this moment, on the other hand, now *that* takes some work.

My clients don't need any help with imagining how things can be different. They have goals and dreams and they know they want them. That's why they've hired me.

The issue is, they don't have a strong handle on their criteria for their success.

Criteria, that's a five dollar word, Leslie - what are you talking about!?

I'm talking about *how* you will measure your success and know when things will be different?

A client said to me the other day, "*I don't know my criteria specifically. Things will just be different!*"

It was an honest response. I loved her for it, but there is a better way to know that you're achieving your professional dreams in the *here and now.*

What is the standard by which you base your choices and recognize their outcomes?

I asked a different client, "What are your criteria of success? How do you know that you're feeling professionally successful?"

She said to me, "I'm making things with my hands, I'm connecting with people, I'm being resourceful, and being creative."

I took her back to an original thought she had about being upset for not being included in a project, but chose, instead, to engage in a volunteer effort. I then asked her, "Are you experiencing all of these things with this project you're doing now?"

"Oh yes!" her eyes lit up.

"Could it be safe to say that there are a million other ways to consistently experience these things that could make you feel happy?" I asked her.

"Of course!" she responded.

At this moment, my client fully understood that success wasn't about having a specific job that would make her feel fulfilled. Success, instead, is consistently fulfilling these personal criteria through a variety of expressions.

She realized by the end of the session, that it didn't matter what her career situation looked like as long as she judged her own success by the ideals she set up for herself and used them to keep her emotions in check.

It all goes back to the question, *"How will you know?"*

Sure, maybe we'll just intuitively know - *I'm happy, yay!*

Sometimes, we don't even realize a good thing until it's gone. Take my personal situation for example:

My husband, Franck, asked me one night about all of my personal and professional challenges that occurred in 2015. It wasn't until I actually listed out everything that I experienced that I realized that I have everything I want: a loving marriage, healthy kids, a peaceful home close to the beach, a fulfilling career, and a sweet car.

In this realization, I said, "I'm 30 years old and have accomplished everything I set out to do and be when I was a kid. Everything else from here on out is the cherry on the cake!"

I almost couldn't believe how good I felt about having acknowledged my accomplishments despite the ups and downs. Just as I was coaching my clients all about recognizing their criteria for success, I realized that I needed reminding of this concept, too.

So, when looking towards your future, think about your own criteria for success.

How will you know - even when things get dark and heavy - that you're on the right path?

Those few little inspiring beams of light will help you navigate your way like a North Star on the darkest, coldest of winter nights and will give you the confidence, peace, and security you need to keep going.

Who knows what will happen in the days and years to come. Even those psychics among us can't even tell for sure. With that said, rely on what makes you feel safe, grounded, and true to tell you what's the best direction to go in. It'll remind you what you're going after, even if sometimes you can't see it.

Questions to Ask Yourself:

1. What are my criteria for success? What are the top 3 to 5 ways I'll know that I'm on the right path and will assure that I'm doing the right thing?

2. Having listed them, can I experience these criteria in a million other ways in the event that I don't get exactly what I want in the upcoming year?

3. Looking back at this past year, do I now realize my criteria? What would they be if they were different from what they are now?

4. Can I name the times when I successfully and consistently met my criteria? What was the situation like? Are things exactly as I wanted them to be? Did I experience happiness anyway?
5. Am I willing to re-evaluate my commitment to my criteria of success?
6. In what ways do my criteria for success reflect my personal values? What are my personal values?
7. Even if I don't know what I specifically want out of my career, do I feel comfortable doing anything as long as I meet my personal criteria of success?

Don't Tell Me About Yourself. Tell Me Your Story.

As a business person, are you struggling to sell yourself?

Do you feel uncomfortable talking about yourself?

Dread having to come up with a list of your personal features and benefits?

All of these things take deep personal insight and self-esteem.

But what if there was a different way? One that was less painful, more rewarding, and clearer from the get go? Why don't you get lost in a story?

Now Leslie, you've gone off the deep end. Get lost in a story?

Yes! Get lost in a story. Look at what you're going through at the moment. All of the confusing and painful twists and turns. They don't make much sense when you're going through it. But, what if you got a chance to peek at the end and everything suddenly made sense? That the moral lesson was made suddenly clear? Look for the "what for?"

When we have the *"what for?"* the whys and hows become all the more clearer.

I ask my clients to look for their *"what for?"* in their life. They come in, stressed to make ends meet, saying that they just want to pay the bills, feel better, stop making the long commute, and stop dreading the people they're around. They want to deal with the plot points instead of the story that sets them up instead.

When you've got something greater to achieve, it makes the plot vehicles that get the star (you) to the next level of character development much more essential and valuable.

So, you say in Example A during an interview: "I am good at photography, graphic design" and ``I'm passionate about skateboarding."

You're just listing qualities, which are obviously clear and defined, but you're missing the "*what for?*"

It's what matters. It's what binds who you are with action. It's what inspires others to join you on the journey (to hire you, work with you, and work for you).

Instead, you could say in Example B, "I believe in telling a visual story of skateboarding because getting an inside look at skaters living their lives their way can inspire others to do the same. So, I take pictures and assemble graphics and tell their stories with these tools. They help advance the sport, bring more people into the culture, and define a personality unique to the brands that I have had the joy of contributing to for the last ten years. Being part of the evolution *and* the revolution excites me and gets me going every day to look at the world with fresh eyes."

Which person would you hire? Example A makes you have to do the work, pull the energy out of yourself to figure out how to use them. Example B, on the other hand, takes you into their world, their story, and intrigues you in such a way that you want to know more about them and the ideas of how to collaborate with them instantly start bubbling within you.

You can feel the pulse in Example B. You see the qualities, the benefits, the hows, and whys. By storytelling, your qualities and benefits reveal themselves in such a subtle way that you don't have to sell them.

By focusing on what you want to accomplish on the grand scale, the means seem to present themselves in a way that you see their value. The circumstances set you up for success, instead of sabotaging your progress.

Are you the victim of circumstance or the master of your life experiences? The first example puts yourself out there, but only does half the work. You're opening yourself up to anything, including those situations that aren't the best suited for you. But, by seeking the value in all experiences and focusing on the overall moral of the story, you control the story's plot and ultimately your role.

Think about your own story.

Do you get caught up in the plot points without looking at their benefit?

Do you talk about yourself as if you were reading off the ingredients section of a cereal box?

Take a deeper look at the journey that you're on. Look for the intrigue, the drama, and examine the character of the most important player - you! Find the *"what for"* and you'll find the *whys* and *hows*.

Your new story begins today.

Write it. Tell it. Share it. Live it.

Questions to Ask Yourself

1. What are the activities I enjoy doing personally and professionally? Explain the "*what for*" for each.

2. Describe how doing my favorite activities fill me and others with positive feelings.

3. What have I used my talents and skills for lately? What were the results?

How Authenticity Creates Memorable Experiences

Productivity is the gift that keeps on giving.

Productivity isn't simply getting a lot done with the fleeting time we have. We all know how "busy" people are often the least productive.

Productivity is a way of examining our impact.

That is, productivity is how we build loyalty through transforming deceptively mundane transactions into custom made opportunities.

George Orwell's philosophy impacted my writing style the most. Through Orwell's essay, *Politics and the English Language*, I took away the lesson to make my writing succinct and to make every word count. Clear communication of an abstract idea in as few words possible is not only a skill, but an art form. This analogy applies to our work activities.

How does your daily performance exhibit skill and grace?

As it's been said, professionals make the complex look easy. Executing repetitive, technical functions while creating impactful, unique experiences is a hallmark of professional mastery.

Everyone does repetitive tasks each day. There are many who focus on productivity as solely a function of time and money.

They often ignore this important question: *How do we make each small, almost meaningless moment memorable and emotionally significant?*

Plant the seeds of an abundance mindset through enhancing customer (relational) experiences. Create personal connections that bear fruit of goodwill long after the experience has passed.

Unfortunately, it is possible to miss the opportunity of seeing how each personal interaction can truly be different and rewarding.

Exceeding experiential expectations through customization is what makes you unique. The word customer literally has the word *custom* in it. Custom for *manner of routine* and custom as in *made to order*. Looking at customers in these two different, yet compatible contexts can redefine how you get things done.

As growing companies focus on scalability there is a tendency to get 'em in and get 'em out. Again, while consistency and repetition are key to branding, customized and personal experiences leave a loyalty building impact.

Ask yourself these questions:

- There may be a hundred other professionals out there who perform the same technical functions as me, but why and how do I make these experiences *memorable* and *unique*?

- What is the *productive* result as a combination of these two elements that differentiate me?

A friend asked me, "Do you get bored by helping people everyday?"

Never!

While the topics of job stresses, marital conflicts, parenting shortcomings, and financial burdens are fundamentally the same on the surface, the way people find their way into and out of their challenges is fascinating. The human experience is endlessly diverse.

Witnessing and facilitating the process by which my clients work their way through pivotal moments in their own ways shows me that every coaching experience can be impactful and unique. This is even when I use the same tools. What my clients takeaway is always personal to them.

Impactful customer experiences are not only productive, they're fruitful; Productive as in meeting specific needs in the most appropriate use of skills, but fruitful because unique relational experiences build trust and loyalty.

See every person as unique, instead of seeing every exchange as the same. When you do, you'll experience how much more productive your work can be. This simple mindset shift can take the same old job and turn it into an ever evolving opportunity of personal expression.

Questions to Ask Yourself:

1. Do I think of my job as, *Same sh*t, different day?* Am I in a rut? What about my role makes me feel that every day is a repetitious hell?

2. How do I make each small, almost meaningless transaction memorable and emotionally lasting for my customers/colleagues/myself?

3. There may be a hundred other professionals out there who do the same technical functions, but why and how do I make these functions memorable and essential? How does the combination of these two elements make me unique?

4. I have specific skills, but those skills aren't who I am. They are just ways that I express my attitude and spirit. What is my attitude? How would I describe my unique presence?

5. Was there ever a time when I approached a repetitive task in a new, fresh way? How were the results different from before? What made the experience different?

Recognize Inspiration and Put It to Work

Breathe in. Exhale. Good.

As easy as it was to do this exercise, so does inspiration come.

A great idea, a stroke of genius, divine intervention; whatever you want to call the experience of capturing an actionable idea. Inspiration touches us all. *How* we act on the ideas we receive is our choice and power. How we exercise our choices communicates who we think we are.

The Qualities of an Inspiring Person

What makes an inspiring person?

It's not someone who sits on or hides great ideas.

Inspiring people are those who get good ideas, recognize them and - more critically - act on them.

There are differing explanations as to where inspiration comes from. But one thing we can all agree on is that inspirational ideas are only as good as how we act on them.

It's pretty easy to answer the question, "What inspires you?"

Take a moment and list a few answers. Pretty natural, huh?

Now, take a moment and ask yourself, "When was the last time I acted on my inspiration?"

Ah… yes. This question takes a minute to answer for many of us.

People have ideas as to what their careers should be like. You, too, have your fair share of ideas. However, what separates leaders from managers is the ability to recognize and consistently act upon inspiration.

Recognizing Inspiration

Receiving ideas and putting them into action on a consistent basis is a skill. Executing ideas requires the ability to discern between bad ideas and good ideas.

Recognizing inspiration usually comes from asking:

- Does this idea help me feel and do better? Or, does this idea make things harder for me or others?
- Am I engaging in this work for solely financial gains or for creating enjoyable experiences?
- Can I act on this idea right now? Is this inspiration positive or does it ask of me to engage in questionable and unethical behavior?

Inspiration affirms your values, encourages you to do and be better, and is instinctively actionable. False ideas usually impose an obligation and cause decision making that results in moral injury.

Consistency: Acting on Inspiration

Recognizing inspiration is Step 1. Action on inspiration is Step 2.

So, you received a good idea and it aligns with your values and vision.

Are you acting on it in a consistent manner? That is, no matter where your inspiration originates and no matter how you choose to express and communicate your ideas, will you and others recognize the consistency in the theme and messages of your results?

Some call this *Personal Branding.* I call it *consistency.*

Evaluate the consistency of true inspiration:

- Does the idea add up with other factors of my life?
- When taking a step back and looking at everything I've done, does this idea make sense?
- What's the pattern? Is it recognizable?

Inspiration Is an Experience That Creates Experiences

Inspiration is an abstract concept and yet its footprint in career development is very real. You can see the result of inspiration in the quality of corporate culture. You can experience the feel and performance of products. You can evoke an emotional response through providing services.

What are the experiential results of inspiration?

- What is my inspiration?
- Where does my inspiration come from?
- And, what values and ideals do I communicate when I act on it?

Choices and their results, when reversed engineered, always communicate the message of an idea.

Look at your latest work. Your inspiration should be clearly expressed and understood.

Look at your portfolio or resume - inspiration is there, too.

What does your body of work consistently say? There, you'll recognize your inspiration in motion.

Inspiration is as only good as the actions that express them. Inspirational humans are those who don't leave their ideals on the shelf, but use them and put them to work.

And finally, true inspiration has a consistent message that creates experiences and emotional responses that are real and measurable. Catch inspiration for yourself, use it, and create something unique and memorable for yourself and others. Inspiration is best when it's put to work.

The Power of Focused Intent

What is focused intent?

Why is focused intent so important even when your life and career seem to make little sense?

> *The master in the art of living makes little distinction between his work and his play, his labor and his leisure, his mind and his body, his education and his recreation, his love and his religion. He hardly knows which is which. He simply pursues his vision of excellence at whatever he does, leaving others to decide whether he is working or playing. To him he is always doing both.*
>
> - L.P. Jacks.

This is one of my favorite quotes. I read it in college and the words have always stuck with me like a mantra or a mandate.

Between going to school full time and working my way through college, I made the decision to do everything I was doing with a vigilance that bordered on the obsessive. I never knew what or how things were going to result from my work. All I knew was that if I did my very best and if I never gave up on myself, then things could only present themselves to me for my highest good. For me, this is what I call focused intent.

Years have gone by and this quote still serves as a reminder to never get caught up in the mire of the small details. The details being dramas, fights, disappointments and the myriad of circumstances that could potentially distract me from my focus.

Rather, focusing on the acts that matter most like a simple hello, a kind embrace, and friendly interactions are what gives our intention power. Shifting your gaze to dwell upon distractions lessens the power of mental force and physical power. So, choose wisely.

Imagine walking down a great, long hall full of doors.

Which one do you choose?

You can feel one in particular calling to you with an odd sense of vibration, movement, or noise coming from behind it.

Out of curiosity you follow it, reaching the door, putting your hand upon the handle and turning it to see what's inside.

Inside is a scenario of your choosing. What is inside is totally up to you, but it's that strange pull you can't explain.

Ask Yourself These Questions:

- *What did I think was waiting for me on the other side of this door?*
- Why did I feel so inclined to go through it?

This is what it feels like to focus our actions on our seemingly inexplicable passions and desires. You focus on something - subconsciously or consciously - and act upon it as if compelled by a strange force.

Gathering what you know about yourself, recognize one important factor in your decision making process: even if you're being pulled to do something, **you can choose** to do it or not and in the **manner** of your choosing.

This is why so many fail to answer the calling of their true nature - or, that professional calling - that asks of us to do something with this powerful drive that lies dormant within us.

Going back to L.P. Jacks: I didn't know *how* I was going to accomplish so much of what I was doing throughout my career. I just felt I had to do it all and I *made the choice* to commit to my vision despite this apparent lack of insight and information on the manner of expression. Looking back at all of the critical moments of my life thus far, I'm just glad that in just about everything I did, I made the commitment to do my best and I did my work well.

If you're unsure about your professional career thus far, and maybe it looks like a hodgepodge of experiences that don't seem to make much sense, then look back at the attitudes you held throughout the journey. These attitudes, or assumptions about your nature, will reveal your intent. Through unveiling your intent, your values and core beliefs will be revealed.

This is how I help my clients reverse engineer their professional experiences when working on their resume and retelling or creating their brand story.

While the devil may be in the details, the intent of our actions always operates from a more remember, enlightened perspective - whether we believe it or not.

As I said before, we sometimes don't know why we do the things we do. When going back and looking at the intent and the focus of your work, there always seems to be an explanation for those who are conscious enough to recognize the patterns.

Ask Yourself These Questions:

- *What is my vision of excellence?*
- What am I saying with what I do?

- What does my work say about who I think I am?
- Even if what you're doing doesn't seem to have a clear end goal or game strategy, imagining that if everything did add up - and it always does - what consistent message would your work say about how you feel about yourself?

Nobody can hold us accountable more than our own selves; we have to be honest with ourselves if we're going to be willing to grow.

Going forward, ask yourself, "Am I doing this activity - even if I don't believe this experience has any immediate or obvious value - to the best of my abilities?"

If the answer is no, then re-examine your intent.

It's not what you think you will get out of your experiences that determines what you put in.

It's what you put into our experiences that determines what you get out of them.

Intention, when examined further, means *to design in mind* through the direction of attention.

Your attitudes design your experiences and the results are the consequences of your attitudes demonstrated through your actions.

So, at the end of the day, what you get out of the experiences doesn't matter as much as the process by which you design them. In layman's terms: the means matter much more than the ends.

So, when you go into "designing" your career, don't get hung up on having it exactly as you think it'll play out. Go into the game with a focused intent of your personal vision of excellence and let that drive your choices. Sure, you'll feel compelled to do many activities, but it's your choice to do them with intention or not.

Trust that the results will play out in the best interests for all involved and most certainly for your highest good. Your awareness in the moment will help you decide what is best for you.

Questions to Ask Yourself:

1. How many times have I looked back at my career with a sense of understanding that I didn't have at the time of the experience? What made the difference? What values can I thank myself for committing to?

2. Do I commit to my different roles with the intent of personal excellence? Why? Why not? What are the stories I tell myself to stop me from doing my very best?

3. Am I consistent in my focus and in my intentions? At what moments have I observed myself falling short of my values? What can my choices reveal about my attitudes?

4. Have I ever gone through a trying or confusing professional period in my life, but look back with a sense of understanding as to *why* I needed to go through the experience? What can that period *and* the results tell me?

5. Do I get caught up in drama, petty fights, and in my own ego? How does that distract from my focus? What positive behaviors enhance my sense of intention or purpose in my career?

GOAL ACHIEVEMENT

Achieve Your Career Passions

Whether your goal is to get into a lifestyle industry or simply make a career change, finding and living your career passion is the cornerstone of building a satisfying professional life.

"But how?" you may ask.

There is a method to the joy of discovering and having a career that's true to you.

Uncovering your career passion is a process of revealing and committing to who you are and what drives you. This process begins by breaking it all down with some very simple questions:

Self-awareness and Exploration

Pursuing your career passion begins by developing self-awareness through exploration.

While you're free to try, it's unnecessary to sit under a tree and meditate until a magical realization suddenly hits you. Instead, start by exploring your motivations and goals to see if they align with your values and priorities.

Questions to Ask Yourself:

1. *What do I have to gain?*
2. *What do I have to express?*
3. *What do I want to create?*

No two careers are alike because two people can have the same job for entirely different reasons.

It's easy to ask what there is to gain from a dream job. However, most only stop there and, ignorantly, build a career on only what they can get instead of the value they can create.

What you have to create includes:

- Your skillset (adaptive and transferable)
- Your knowledge base (hands on experience)
- Formal and informal education
- Personal gifts and interests (like vision and ideals)

Knowing your value makes for streamlined job searches, stress free networking and interviewing, and fruitful salary negotiations.

Questions to Ask Yourself:

1. *What am I trying to get away from?*
2. *What do I want more of?*

It seems like asking the same question twice, but the purpose is to establish both negative and positive perspectives.

Asking what you're trying to get away from gets you to look at:

- What attitudes and experiences drag you down

- What kinds of routines and behaviors need to stop
- The reasons why you hate your current work situation

By asking yourself what you want more of, you're creating a values-based vision that helps you be specific about your goals.

A sample answer includes, "I want to work with people who care about what they do, design sustainable surf products, and incorporate a professional and personal life that works for me and my family."

Questions to Ask Yourself:

1. *What are my short term goals?*
2. *What are my long term goals?*

Answering this question can be tough, because when put on the spot, people say, "I don't know!"

The long and short of it usually involves, *I want to make money and I want to like what I do.*

Ask yourself, "What specific results can I achieve to let me know that I have successfully created my vision?"

Acting as guideposts, goals are changeable and flexible, so don't get hung up on whether or not you achieve them. Rather, goals serve as the motivation and inspiration needed to face fears and deal with the psychological barriers that keep you from making career passions into realities.

Assessing Risk and Overcoming Barriers

Before developing a clear vision and a plan for finding and achieving career passions, first take stock in available resources and assess your readiness, determination, and fears.

Questions to Ask Yourself:

1. *What are my internal barriers?*
2. *What are my external barriers?*

Internal and external barriers prevent identification and achievement of career passions.

There are different kinds of internal barriers:

- **Psychological:** moods, attitudes, and assumptions
- **Behavioral:** habits and choices
- **Vocational:** Formal education, experience, knowledge

With internal barriers, it may be necessary to examine them and deal with them (like working with a coach, psychologist, or a trusted confidant or mentor) as you simultaneously create an authentic career.

As for vocational internal barriers, you might, for example, have to go back to school or take on a learning position like an internship or assistant position to cover any profile gaps.

External barriers are present conditions that you can work around or change.

Examples include:

- Insufficient income to go back to school
- Living in a location without relevant jobs
- Lacking the emotional or social support to pursue career goals

External barriers can be either beyond or within our control, but nonetheless require imagination to creatively transform them into opportunities.

Questions to Ask Yourself:

1. *What are my resources?*
2. *What are my opportunities?*

Instead of focusing only on what you don't have and what you need, take stock of resources that can open up doors to discovering and achieving your career passions.

Resources, for example, can include:

- Tapping into your personal and professional networks and industry organizations
- Industry publications
- Educational opportunities found at your job or in your local community (e.g. company sponsored education or industry related volunteer opportunities)

Questions to Ask Yourself:

1. *What is my risk tolerance?*
2. *Do I trust myself?*
3. *Do I trust life?*

Go gung-ho or take it one small step at a time

Life's complications can deter you from answering your calling, but they don't have to if your goals and objectives are broken down into manageable steps.

Do you have a family to care for? Are they on board for drastic change or do you need to make a smooth transition? Or, are you just starting out in your career and can couch surf until you realize your goals?

Either way, you can accomplish your goals if you know how you and those dependent on you can handle risk and change as you walk your path.

By identifying motivations, interests and values and working with what already exists in your life (the good, the bad, and the ugly) you're better equipped to take manageable steps.

Breaking down objectives daily, weekly, and annually (while being flexible with who you are and with what is going on) can turn abstract desires into a concrete reality.

Committing To Yourself and Rediscovering Your Passions

Not all of us get that *ah-ha!* moment where we wake up knowing exactly what we should do with our lives and how it should all be done. And finding your career passion isn't a discovery that happens just once in your life.

After a while, it's possible to reach the end of a chapter and feel the desire to begin a new incarnation of passion. By committing to yourself through action - recognizing what you want to create and achieve and by doing what it takes to continually overcome what stands in your way - you can awaken and sustain your career passion on a daily basis.

Set Career Goals For the Right Reasons

You have an idea as to what you'd like to experience in life.

Your career goals fit within the scope of your life dreams often because what you do affords you the means to experience your overarching personal goals. It can be hazy to distinguish what your career goals actually look like because a fine line between personal goals and professional aspirations exists.

I encourage you to take a step back to see the subtle differences and interconnectedness between career goals and personal goals. Through this exploration, you'll achieve a greater understanding that can empower you to make more informed and satisfying choices.

Career goals, similar to financial goals, often fulfill or take us a step closer to our personal goals.

For example, if you want to travel the world and collect the world's largest magnet collection, a job might help you achieve that. Maybe, you want to reach or surpass a financial goal. A job or business can fulfill that or take you a step closer to that goal. Maybe, you want to be home every night to feed and tuck in your babies. Again, your work can help you create certain conditions to make your personal vision possible.

Your career is not something that exists within a vacuum - it's a living, breathing expression of you in motion.

I have learned from my experience that nobody wants to be CEO "just because." There always exists an underlying personal motivation which explains why people commit to long and challenging processes. *Unless, you're some glutton for suffering and, even then, you've got something deep going on there!*

My top three long term career goals are:
1.
2.
3.

By meeting these three career goals, I'd like to achieve the following personal goals:
1.
2.
3.

This exercise may sound abstract.

You might say, "Yeah right, Leslie, like I know exactly what I want to do with my career, let alone my life. I don't even know where I'll be getting next month's mortgage payment! Let's focus on that, please!"

I've been there. I have.

I remember a moment in my life when I literally had *sixty cents* in my bank account! For many of us, our career goals are usually determined by our financial situation. But, I warn, there is mental slavery in this kind of thinking and perception of life. My goal is to help you set yourself free... Stay with me...

When I ask my clients what they really want outside of the scope of doing a job to get money, the answers are usually foggy and the present opportunities are usually limited. However, when we explore the higher ideals and desired experiences, clients usually see a shift in their career goals, both in the long and short term. The "shoulds" and "have-to's" merely become choices within a plethora of possibilities.

Often, my clients realize through this exploration that they don't need as much as they initially believed they needed to live happily and to achieve their goals. Even more importantly, they realize that they're more capable than they initially believed and have more freedom as the choices begin to appear.

Career goals are only as limited to what we perceive as our overarching life goals. Take the story of Mike Tobia, former Head of Product and Marketing for Dragon, as an example of this concept:

I sat down with Mike for an episode of #DRIVE. Mike had this to say about career goals, "Life is constantly evolving and changing. I think it's important for people to have goals and work towards them and I'm learning in life you need to be flexible as well."

Mike learned this lesson the hard way.

In a bizarre metaphor of flexibility, Mike broke his back in a life changing snowboarding accident leaving him to witness his career as a professional snowboarder slip away from his fingertips. Going from a pro-snowboarder to wondering if he'd ever walk again, Mike's perspective of *his* life changed in an instant. And, as a result, so did his outlook on his career.

Learning to walk again, he also took steps in a new professional direction which led to amazing contributions to Dragon and Nike, innovating and shaping the *way we see through* visual products forever.

After taking a deeper look at how your career transforms as a result of your greater life understandings, you can see that, when it comes to planning our careers, how you've got to identify the overarching vision that drives your seemingly insignificant career decisions.

Your career fit within the ecosystem of your life. People can live without careers (toddlers and teenagers prove this point), but we cannot have careers without our lives.

Taking insights from Mike Tobia's inspiring story, draw your own links between what you want to achieve with your life and how your career helps you do that.

Questions to Ask Yourself:

1. What are my career goals? How do they help me fulfill, or take a step closer to, my personal life goals?

2. Do I make career decisions based on temporary financial circumstances? How does this way of thinking help me and how does it limit my choices?

3. How are my career goals integrated into my personal vision? How do my personal visions affect my career decisions?

4. When was the last time I was faced with a life changing challenge? How did the direction of my career shift as a result? How did it serve me in the long term?

5. If I could achieve my personal life goals without the traditional concept of a job, how would I do it? How would I make my own version of a career? What would those goals be?

Defining Your Version of Success

Success. It has so many definitions.

Depending on your culture and your upbringing, what success looks and feels like could be totally different than what I believe success to be.

The most important question when it comes to the discussion of success and achievement is, "How will you know when you are a success?"

This simple question forces us to examine what we believe about success, how much of our attitudes are preprogrammed by our culture and conditioning, and how attainable success really is.

This question alone can break our perceptions as to what *we can* conceive and achieve.

Conceiving | Believing | Achieving

Napoleon Hill said, "Whatever your mind can conceive and believe, it can achieve regardless of how many times you have failed in the past."

There are times in our lives where our perception of ourselves has become so narrow, so dulled and hazy that we can't even stretch our minds to conceive, as in imagine, ourselves and our lives being any different than what it has historically been.

You walk, hypnotized into an oddly comfortable, yet disserving self-concept of self-sabotage, missing opportunities that present themselves all around you.

My first job as a coach is to change how you see your nature and therefore what you can do and, as a result, experience.

You might say to me, "Now, wait a minute, Leslie. I imagine great things for myself all of the time: the new house, the dream spouse, and the great job! I get you, we've all been told to focus on what we want as that's how we achieve these experiences."

True, true. But bear with me, we're just halfway there...

What if you could re-examine all of the real reasons why you believe you need something and, by doing so, you realize that you can attain desired experiences through a variety of means? The point is, when you examine your *whys*, the *hows* seem to become much easier to conceive.

Take a client who tells me, "I need a new job because I don't get paid enough and it doesn't challenge me anymore."

Good. Why?

"Because I don't have enough money to travel and I need new professional challenges so that I can feel valued."

Why do you need to travel and feel valued at your work?

"Because I need a constant sense of change, newness, and adventure and I want to know that my life will make a difference along the way."

This conversation can go on and on. And, guess what? I bet you can already think of ways that this client can explore and experience new horizons and get a sense of personal fulfillment just by this short conversation alone.

Perhaps this client ends up getting a new job as a travel guide in a different country. Perhaps they manage to achieve a management position where they get paid to travel. Or, maybe this person quits their job and works for the Peace Corps instead. Who knows!? This exercise is meant to challenge our ability to conceive different possibilities.

Conceiving new possibilities comes by challenging old beliefs and paradigms.

Why? How? What if? If I did know, what would I know?

People accept their beliefs as the rules of the game and we must play by them if we are to get what we want out of life.

In the words of Dwight Schrute, "False!"

Fact: You can change "the rules" - your beliefs - at any time. This alone changes the playing field of possibilities. Who says you have to do things *this* way?

Challenging old paradigms and breaking through them offers a renewed sense of purpose and belief in yourself. That "Yes I can!" moment. *I can totally go for that promotion! I can definitely be seen at work operating in a different capacity than I am now. I can trust myself to start a company. Not only can I, but I believe I can!*

So, when you're sitting down with your list of goals and thinking about how you'll go about making your life a success, examine for a moment what success really means and what you really need to feel happy, safe, and appreciated at work and in life.

Ask yourself some key questions: How will I really know when I have achieved success? How will it feel? What will it take? Do I really need to do it *this* way? What if I tried it another way?

Success.

Conceive it and believe it.
You can and will achieve it.

Questions to Ask Yourself:

1. Thinking quickly, what have I been wanting to achieve lately? List two to three things.

2. How will I know when I have achieved success? What will it look like, feel like, sound like?

3. Why do I need to achieve these things? Are they necessary for true happiness, safety, and love?

4. When did I suddenly believe that I had to experience these things? What was I really trying to get for myself at the moment of conceiving that idea?

5. What are the unwritten rules to the game for me to achieve my goals? For example, do I have to stay at this job for x amount of time? Do I have to put up with a mean boss? Do I have to live in this city? What are the things we believe we have to do/experience/have before we get that success?

6. What if I could change the rules and achieve my vision of success, and still enjoy the experience, in a different way?

7. How does my action plan look different now, having asked myself these aforementioned questions?

Three Career Planning Mistakes to Avoid

How will you give away your life?

This question sounds pretty dramatic, doesn't it? But that's how the world measures a lifetime - through time. You put a value on that time and hope that whatever it is you get out of it is equal to or greater than the effort you put out.

And, when it comes to career planning it's no wonder that the concepts mentioned above make it, at times, debilitating and paralyzing. As children, we fantasize about the roles we'll get to play: the rescuer, the caretaker, the giver, the advisor, etc. But then, as we get older, we learn that there are so many implications that not only make career planning a touchy subject, but one that is hard to wrap our minds around.

The good news is it doesn't have to be so frightening or confusing. Direction comes from knowing where we are at now on the career map and understanding how we got here. This, as simple as it seems, is where all the inner conflict begins. Here's why:

Reason No. 1: Failing to Quantify Your Value

It's hard to quantify what you give versus what you receive. And, people who can do this seem to have all the luck in getting what they want. When I am with clients, I ask them to quantify their experience in a specific and measurable way. The question is: *How did things improve as a result of your specific contribution?*

Why do most resumes look depressing and unappealing? Because people put more emphasis on what they do instead of why and how. For what purpose and to what end? Can't answer that question? Believe me, you're not alone.

When you are aware of the value you create, you're comfortable asking for what you need - and more.

The inability to communicate the value of the past experiences creates a foggy future. This brings me to part two.

Reason No. 2: Failing to Connect the Past with the Present

How does it all add up? Can't do your own math? Don't expect others to do it for you.

As an expert in resume and portfolio construction, I can see the story of the career and how it all adds up. People from all over the world ask me to look at their resumes because they need this perspective. This lack of perspective is expensive because it costs future opportunities and present career happiness.

Where is the need?
Where were the struggles and growth opportunities?
And where were the breakthroughs?

The answers to these questions tie together in a cohesive way. Without tying your experiences together you can sell yourself short because of the disjointed view of your experiences and ultimately of yourself.

Those who do not understand their past are doomed to repeat it. Career planning is about creating new experiences - not about reliving old ones that have lost their flavor.

Reason No. 3: Failing to See Your Own Inherent Value

With that said, lacking a full understanding of the value you created during past and present experiences lowers self-esteem. Without a high self-esteem, you're less inclined to take risks, and express yourself.

It's like trying to sell something without knowing why it's useful and how it works. You are on the journey of recognizing your own inherent value so that others see it, too. Some people see their past experiences as a string of failures while others see steps along the path of personal growth. If you were hiring, which camp would you bet on to grow your business?

Taking steps to honor your growth experiences and glean the valuable insight and wisdom from them is key to developing self-confidence. The self-confidence that stems from a deep sense of personal value and wisdom attained to apply to future situations is what makes career planning easier and dare I say, joyful and exciting. Knowing where you've been and where you are now - and, more importantly, why - creates a peace that few have the pleasure of knowing. And it's peace of mind that makes deciding what to experience next a fundamental cornerstone of developing new professional horizons.

When thinking about the future, take a moment to reflect on all of the resources you've unlocked within you and the value that you have created in every experience. This is the launching point for future success because knowing your worth and believing in yourself today means that you are willing to bet on yourself today for a bright tomorrow.

Questions to Ask Yourself:

1. When I think about planning my career do I feel overwhelmed, scared, or nervous? Where does this feeling come from? What can it tell me about what I need to know now in order to move forward?

2. Am I able to quantify the value I created in past professional experiences? Can I specifically tell potential business partners/employers how I have made a difference as a result of my work?

3. Knowing the specific, measurable value that I offer my industry, am I paid less than, equal to, or greater than the value that I give? How can I assure equal compensation for my contribution?

4. Do I understand my professional history? Do I rely on others to do that job for me? What does my professional journey say about my choices and beliefs? Is there anything that needs to be emphasized or changed in order to move forward?

5. Do I feel confident to communicate my inherent value and wisdom attained from my growth experiences? What key areas of knowledge can I pass down? How does my contribution make a difference?

6. Would I objectively bet on myself based on my ability to communicate my value and tell my story? Why or why not?

Smart Career Goals

Do you ever feel that you're off your career track?

Do you ever feel that you're constantly changing your mind about things because you're not getting the results you expect?

Do you feel that your life isn't going the way you've planned and you feel totally lost?

Check out seven strategies to master your career goals so you can get focused and back on track.

I. Prioritize

Make a list of the activities that you enjoy doing, what really matters, including the things that make you feel like a million bucks. Focus more on experiencing what matters to you. Eliminate unhealthy distractions and behaviors.

Questions to Ask Yourself:

1. What are my top life priorities?
2. What activities increase my energy?
3. What behaviors or distractions are keeping me from accomplishing goals?

4. Who can help me resolve inner conflicts and eliminate unhealthy behaviors?
5. Can I make it my goal to resolve emotional conflicts on the path of achieving my goals?

II. Rehash Forgotten Goals

Remember the original goals that you've set for yourself, but you just kept putting off or felt too afraid to accomplish?

Do you have a passion that keeps popping up in your mind, no matter how hard you try to push them aside?

Write them down and acknowledge them.

Questions to Ask Yourself:

1. What kind of passions or goals have I forgotten or ignored that keep speaking to me?
2. What stories do I tell myself that rationalize procrastination?

III. Acknowledge Your Fears and Worries

You can't move past fears until we've acknowledged them and dealt with them. Most of the time, the chances of your worst fears coming true are highly improbable. Work your way out of the fear with someone you trust, so that you don't spend your precious energy fighting them away.

Questions to Ask Yourself:

1. What issues from my past or present that I need to overcome in order to gain the confidence to go into the experiences that fulfill my goals?
2. What is the first small step I can take to overcome them?

3. What undesirable moods prevent me from feeling good?

IV. Let Go Of Expectations

Don't worry about having things work out or appear a certain way.

Most people are too busy worrying about themselves to notice your failures or insecurities. Circumstances work out to reveal your attitudes. *Trust in your intuition rather than your expectations.*

Questions to Ask Yourself:
1. When was the last time my intuition led me in the right direction?
2. What does my intuition say about my goals?
3. What have my experiences revealed about my attitudes?

V. Get Real About the Commitment

If you know that in order to become a rocket scientist, you've got to study a lot of science, then hit the books and do everything you can to accomplish it.

Take stock of your current talents, strengths, and weaknesses and develop a manageable plan to expand your knowledge.

Questions to Ask Yourself:
1. What are the current obstacles that I need to overcome?
2. Who can give me information (by research or informational interviews) that I need to know to make a decision?
3. Am I committed to my goals?
4. Am I committed to being honest with myself at every step of the journey?

VI. Focus On Authentic Connections

Focus on being compassionate, understanding, and connected to the people around you.

The more you connect with others in authentic ways, the more they notice and good things start to happen. Communicate your goals and purpose with authenticity and you'll see the more willing others are to help you meet your goals.

Questions to Ask Yourself:

1. Who supports me and my goals?
2. Do they know about my goals?
3. Do I focus more on what I can get rather than what I can give?
4. Can I express myself safely?
5. Is my network psychologically safe?

VII. Judge Yourself Less

You are your harshest critic. Give yourself some compassion and learn to breathe. The more you enjoy the ride and the less time you spend criticizing yourself, the more fulfilled you will be.

Questions to Ask Yourself:

1. What activities can I do to love myself and give myself a break?
2. What negative self-talk do I say about myself?
3. Is my mind psychologically safe?
4. Do I feel good in my body?

Re-examining your career goals with some simple questions. Work on recognizing how attitudes and choices speed up or slow down progress.

Give yourself the motivation and compassion necessary to keep moving forward one day and one step at a time.

What Is Your Leadership Plan?

You just so happen to be next in line for a promotion and it's your turn to take the torch of responsibility in order to go further than your predecessor.

Sounds like a lot of pressure, doesn't it?

Believe me, I get you. So take my experience of coaching successors so you can hit the ground running.

Many only think of the prestige and the benefits to be gained from a promotion, thinking, *"Ooh, what will I do with my bonus check? A nice vacation, maybe?"*

You haven't been on the job longer than a hot minute and you're already thinking about a vacation? It's time to switch gears and get into a higher perspective - a more *enlightened* perspective - about leadership.

When it comes to succession planning, I'm charged with assuring the person who is going to get promoted does a couple of things:

A) Not undo the good works have already been established and **B)** have a plan that reflects he or she does indeed have a sound mind and truly merits the responsibility - not just because they're "next in line."

Succession planning is a twofold process: **1)** Getting the candidate mentally and emotionally primed for the job and **2)** Assuring their plan for the future of this position lines up with the organizational goals and values that are in place.

Part 1) Getting Primed For Success

When I think of preparing for a promotion, I see the montage of Rocky Balboa training for his big fight, finally running up the stairs of Philadelphia's Museum of Art, feeling strong and ready to take on the challenge. This is where the mental battle begins: on the training ground.

Promotion isn't just about the money or prestige, it's about the commitment, responsibility, humility, and wisdom exercised in balance with the needs of others. Taking a look at ourselves and examining our attitudes about leadership is paramount to the process of promotions.

Questions to Ask Yourself:

1. Am I a "do as I say, not as I do" kind of boss? Do I actually listen to my colleagues, subordinates, and the public?
2. Am I hungry for power and control or do I serve and lead to empower?
3. Another one that I pick up on with executives is: Do I qualify people based on what they can do for me?
4. Am I judgemental?

It's my job to strip away arrogant attitudes to assure that when it comes time to make a critical decision for the company, they don't have their head shoved so far up where the sun doesn't shine that they make costly and even irreversible mistakes. This includes making poor forecasts, alienating the team, dropping the ball on deliverables, and breaching their duty of loyalty. Attitude and insight determine whether or not a successor is worthy of the promotion and the service they'll render to key stakeholders.

Part 2) Having a Good Leadership Plan
I have seen new CEOs get booted in just a few months because they didn't capture the hearts and minds of their stakeholders - especially their employees.

Failure to connect boils down to failing to have a plan to build meaningful connections. This is just one of the ways a successor can drop the ball and waste time, if not temporarily reverse progress.

Having a solid plan to overcome the challenges of a newly promoted leader is par for the course. There are opportunities to build connections everywhere: disgruntled employees, poor sales performance, logistical nightmares, PR crises, and the list goes on.

A successor who is not only well-researched and aware of their impending responsibilities to help repair what is broken and lead their team into the unknown demonstrates a level of emotional mastery and leadership consciousness that few have successfully reached.

Key stakeholders (employees, partners, board members, owners, and consumers) want to know for certain that a successor truly knows what he or she is doing, not just going through the motions.

So, whether you're in consideration for a promotion or just earned one, consider these two essential questions:

1. What are your attitudes and perspectives about leadership?

    And,

2. Do you have a clear demonstration of business aptitude as defined by a general, if not specific, plan that is aligned with the pressing needs and values of your key stakeholders?

New responsibility is just that, a responsibility. Because, we're not our job, our job is defined by us.

So, if you've got your head up your rear end and think you'll just bully your way to success, you've got another thing coming: unemployment. Clarifying and working in line with more enlightened priorities are the natural fuel that can take your performance to a whole new level.

Questions to Ask Yourself:

1. What are my strengths and weaknesses as a leader? What errors in judgment did the person before me make and where did they succeed? What are the key takeaways from their wins and losses?
2. What are the unhealthy attitudes that hurt me as a leader? Do I qualify people? Am I judgemental? Am I fair and do I listen?
3. What is my true motivation for this promotion? The responsibilities and the difference I can make or the benefits such as money and prestige?
4. What are the current struggles of my predecessor? What advice can they glean from their experience? What wisdom can I leave behind for the person who is taking my job?
5. What key initiatives will I have to take on immediately upon taking the post? Who are the key stakeholders that I have to prove myself to?

Be Proud of What You've Done

When thinking back on past career experiences, there's a tendency to look back and focus on mistakes and negative experiences.

It's easy to look back and say, "What good can possibly come out of this?"

When working with clients, I ask them to reflect on their career thus far. It's not a platitude when I say *We are our own harshest critics.* When reflecting upon your career for this current year, be kind to yourself and take the role of the cheerleader - even just for a moment - to thank yourself for all that you've accomplished. Take stock on just how productive you really are.

Just yesterday, a career coaching client shared his feelings of regret and jealousy over his younger sibling's professional success.

The question he raised was, "Why do we have two different careers when we share the same (difficult) personal background?"

I eventually posed the reflection, "How is this statement true when you practically raised your sibling on your own? Your sibling had *you* to guide and protect him."

Driving the point home, I said, "You didn't have that luxury of having someone looking out for your success. Do you realize that you raised a successful adult?"

My client was taken aback.

He had never considered his challenging life experiences in such a way. Nor did he congratulate himself on shaping the future of his sibling in a positive way.

His eyes widened. His face lightened and he said, "I have never thought about it in that way."

You see, in the cloudy mindset of comparison, of seeing lack, and of expectations, we fail to acknowledge what is: the goodness in our hearts, the instinctive positive action that guides us to the right people and places at the right time, and the inexplicable and even mundane miracles of our lives.

Like Scrooge, we can take so much of our lives and careers for granted. Not out of malice, but out of hurt and fear - from having been burned in the past or anxious about bad things happening in the future.

"You just want to survive," as so many of my clients say when they first meet me.

Not enough credit goes to the good things around us and certainly not enough credit goes to our positive qualities and actions and the potential that lies latent within ourselves. You will eventually realize that loving and honoring yourself is the prerequisite to loving and honoring our careers.

Some have said to me, "If I can just have a good paying job that lets me do what I love in the new year, then I'll have time to love and take care of myself."

This is how we set ourselves up for disappointment.

Begin by taking stock of all of the great things you've accomplished this year.

List the resources that lie ready to be awakened within you and those that you've used thus far.

Identify the source of your assumptions and attitudes. Through the process of taking stock, you'll begin to feel differently about the conditions of your life. More importantly, how you see yourself will change, too.

Questions to Ask Yourself:

1. What are my career fears? Where do they come from? What is the assumption of those fears that try to keep me from getting hurt again?

2. What impact have I made in my career this past year? What were the challenges, the opportunities to truly be my best self, and how did things change as a result?

3. Who have I made a positive impression on? How did their work/lives/experience change as a result?

4. What resources within myself did I discover that I have to turn stressful situations into learning opportunities? What are they?

5. What were the top 3 accomplishments I experienced at work and in life? What makes these accomplishments so special?

Wax On, Wax Off: Finding, Nurturing, and Being Mentors

You don't have to be a karate kid to have a wise mentor that'll teach you self-mastery.

By asking yourself the right questions, you will see that mentors are there, all around, gently fine tuning us into better people every day.

From my personal stories to aspirational figures like pro snowboarders Kelly Clark and Chloe Kim, mentoring can be the rising tide that lifts all boats taking the collective from good to great.

Discover how you can recognize your mentors, nurture these relationships, and how to be one yourself.

Mentors: My Stories

While living in France, I was required to get an internship with a professional to learn French in a professional context.

The person who I would work under would act as a mentor, helping me learn business French and what it's like to work in France.

For my project, I asked a woman who runs workshops for job seekers and she agreed. However, days before the internship was to begin she brought me into her office and said, "I can't take you as an intern. I'll be sharing with you my business practices and I don't want you to copy me when you go out on your own."

I was shocked by her distrust, but that little voice inside said, "Don't try to convince her to take you on. Just get up, thank her for her time, shake her hand, and walk away."

I did just that and with the help from the program director I found an internship at AFPA, France's national vocational school, and my mentors there exposed me to the new world of coaching and training in Europe. And, our relationships naturally grew into long standing friendships and collaborative exchanges.

Fast forward: I'm back in the U.S.A., working on re-establishing my coaching business.

Through my network, I set up different explorational meetings with different pros to see if they could become networking partners. In one meeting, I clicked with a woman in my field who totally understands my professional values, loves what I am doing to help people, and sees my potential. Gradually, she started introducing me to people, giving me advice on how to market myself, how to improve my chances in business and regularly following up with me and my family. In fact, I didn't realize she acted as a mentor until Chad at Malakye asked me to share this advice.

How To Recognize Your Mentor

If you really take the time to think about it, you presently have or have had mentors.

It's unnecessary to go up to a stranger and say, "Will you be my mentor?" Although, you can!

Sometimes, we can have more than one mentor - spiritual, professional, hobbies - who teach and guide us in a variety of ways. The trick is to ask the questions that help us realize mentors are actually all around us. Moms, dads, friends, neighbors, old and new bosses, professors - mentors are everywhere.

Questions to Ask Yourself:

1. Who do I know that takes a sincere interest in me and my projects and helps me find ways to move forward?
2. Does this person try to control my thinking or help me grow and open my mind?
3. Does this person go out of their way to spend time with me? When thinking about our time together, what have I learned?
4. What were the turning points in my career and life? Who were the influential people who made a difference? How?

Nurturing the Mentor-Mentee Relationship

It's easy to take advantage of the ones who care about our careers the most.

Bad follow up, getting free advice without offering anything in return, and not showing respect or enthusiasm for our mentor's help. Failing to appreciate mentors can burn bridges fast. Without realizing it, mentees lose the support they never realized they had in the first place.

Mentoring relationships are reciprocal and nurturing. Mentorships are not all *me first, gimme, gimme!* Ask yourself how you are being of service to your mentor and if you're genuinely interested in them as people or if you just have an ulterior motive.

Another way to maximize the mentor-mentee relationship is to be clear about your goals. Specific goals help our mentors zoom into identifying solutions to problems. Chances are, they've gone through our specific situation and can help from their experience and once we've gone through it, they'd be pleased to hear how their advice or assistance helped you achieve your goals.

Questions to Ask Yourself:

1. Am I clear about my goals, struggles, and questions? What are they?
2. How am I helping my mentor? Do I offer anything to them that they can value?
3. Am I following up on a regular basis and how am I saying, "Thanks! I appreciate you!"?

Paying It Forward: Being a Mentor

The cool thing about being authentic ourselves is that we've got a unique way of experiencing and doing things.

You've also got your own history and lessons that can help advance the efforts of others. When I was at Mammoth snowboarding one day, I thought about snowboarders Kelly Clark and Chloe Kim's mentor-mentee relationship.

Clark said this about mentoring,

> I realized in the last few months that I am not here to get anything anymore. I am here to contribute to the sport. It is no secret that some of these women will do tricks or will take the sport to a place where I never could. But I am going to take it as far as I can and hand it off. (Glass, 2015)[5]

---

[5] http://www.forbes.com/sites/alanaglass/2015/03/08/how-kelly-clark-devin-logan-snowboard-and-ski-by-the-golden-rule/

When asked about Clark, Chloe Kim had this to say about their relationship:

> You're at all the contests together. She helps me out so much. She's an amazing mentor and an amazing snowboarder. She always inspires me. (Foltz, 2015)[6]

The inspirational relationship of these women is just one story out of many in this world where mentoring can not only advance yourself, but the collective. Take a look inside yourself and see what you have to offer a mentee.

Questions to Ask Yourself:

1. What life or work experiences have taught me the most in life? How can I share them to benefit others?
2. What have my mentors taught me? What inspirational messages can I pass on?
3. What issues do people constantly come to me about? Is there a theme and if so, what is it?

Either by being a mentee or a mentor, each person has so much to give and gain.

All you have to do is look around and see them there, nurture the relationships and pass along the wisdom when it's your turn to teach. Take it from me and don't let the short sightedness of others fool you: there is nothing to lose by mentoring - there is everything to gain! Wax included.

---

[6] http://www.summitdaily.com/news/15335610-113/kelly-clark-chloe-kim-and-arielle-gold-leading-charge-in

Three Strategies For Staying Focused on Your Goals

If you're lucky to have gotten to the point of figuring out what you want to do with your career, now is the time to stand up and ride the mountain.

Having taken position, there seems to be a moment in which we second guess ourselves and go, "Oh snap, maybe I wasn't ready to charge after all!"

That's when distraction and procrastination start to rear their ugly, unproductive heads.

No fear! There's a way to stay focused and strong.

Taking off on a new project - whether at work or making a career move - is an exciting step.

But what happens when the sheen of novelty and excitement wears off and we're left with the stark reality of hard work and commitment? Following through is like a coyote ugly experience after the previous night's beer goggles have worn off: you just want to chew off your arm and call it a loss. But you can't and you mustn't because you're better than that and there has got to be a way to stay committed and focused on what can seem to be a daunting and overwhelming project.

1. Staying in the Now: If Not Now, When?

You don't have to believe in *The Power of Now*[7] to know that all we've got is right now to get things done.

I've seen some of my own clients leave a session super pumped and focused on their project, but when they think about all of the work, struggle, and challenges they might have to confront on the way to their goals they lose steam. It happens to the best of us because dwelling on the unknowns can be overwhelming. The unknown is a place of anxiety - don't go there; Stay grounded in the power of your own presence.

Thinking about the unknown and anticipating failure, confrontation, and challenges does nothing but fill the mind with worry about how things *should* turn out instead of what we *can* do in the here and now.

It's not a cliche when they say the present is a gift because it's a place of power: The power of now comes from knowing we have choices right now that can and will determine the outcome of present events.

2. Let Yourself Soar: Stop Holding Yourself Back

When a client comes to see me, I intuitively pick up on their highest potential and I happen to see great potential in all of my clients.

The challenge with staying focused on goals is not so much about getting sucked into weaknesses, but rather the act of shying away from the greatness that lies dormant within. Why?

Because being the very best and highest version ourselves requires great self-discipline, insight (in-sight, as in looking within to see our inner truth) and generous self-acceptance.

---

[7] The Power of Now book by Eckhart Tolle

Surprisingly, many people are not ready to commit to that kind of relationship: The relationship with the self!

So, when you hear self-doubt and critical self-talk like, "Who am I to think I could do such an amazing thing?" give yourself the benefit of the doubt. Allow yourself the opportunity to surprise yourself. Believe in your inherent capacity for thinking, acting, and being better than you thought before. Allow experiences to help you appreciate your own authenticity. You can stay on track and aligned with your highest career vision.

3. Look Where You Want to Go: Not Just Good Snowboarding Advice

Last week, a friend of mine in the snowboarding industry made his way over from Denver for a family style meal at our home. We got to talking about career building and maximizing life as we ate. We talked about many ideals on the subject, but what he said about focus jumped out and stuck with me:

> "The way I see it (the career) is like when you're snowboarding: wherever you keep your eyes is where you'll end up going. Look towards the trees and you'll end up in the trees. It's a pretty simple way to explain it, but it makes sense to me."

This, folks. This.

Keeping your "eyes" or focus on where you want to go in your career helps the body (conscious and subconscious mind) to act on that intention. Typically, you intuitively know what to do in most situations (like snowboarding, in my friend's example), so practice allowing yourself to do what you do best under the guidance of a crystal clear vision of yourself.

3. Focus: Mindfully Putting It All Together

Once you've got a crystal clear vision or goal for your career, you've suddenly placed ourselves into a mental battlefield.

It means fighting for territory in your mind as to what will take focus: anxieties and expectations of the future, doubt and insecurity, and distraction. Or, being fully engaged in the present, committed to being your best self, and maintaining crystal clear visions.

Putting the effort into being focused and concentrated takes effort before it can totally be natural and second nature, but it's worth the practice for perfecting self-mastery and professional performance.

You don't have to be a guru to be focused, you just have to know that your greatest career potential lies within your own hands: Focus lies within the eyes of the beholder.

Questions to Ask Yourself:

1. Do I focus my attention more on barriers than opportunities?
2. Do I allow negative self-talk discourage me or paralyze my mind?
3. What is the script that runs in my head when I think about my goals?
4. Do I accept present limitations? What if these limitations can't actually stop me from fulfilling my goals?

JOB SEARCHING

The Shmooz: Chad on Blazing Your Own Career Path

Leslie and Chad during a job search group circle during a Shmooz event in Long Beach, California.

I sat next to Chad in a Career Strategy group discussion. It was our first time facilitating a group together and I have to say, listening to Chad talk was like sitting in group therapy.

Chad Mihalick and the Malakye crew switched up the format at a Shmooz event at Agenda Trade Show in Long Beach one year. Instead of a panel discussion, there were three rotating discussion groups each based on a single topic.

Dozens of unemployed and actively seeking listeners filed in and listened for anything new or different that could influence their career decisions. They were hoping for anything they haven't heard or seen online before that could give them the paradigm switching advice they were so hungry for.

It takes a certain amount of humility to come to a Shmooz event. Attendees put themselves out there as professionally packaged as can be and, to a certain level, raw and vulnerable. All the while - in the face of uncertainty - putting their best face forward in hopes of landing an opportunity with one of the companies hiring at the event. As some are confident in their job prospects, there hangs a subtle, yet perceivable veil of desperation, bitterness, and hope.

Chad Mihalick sees this.

As founder of Malakye.com he understands how discouraging, hopeless, and confusing the job search (and selling ourselves) can be. He, as a leader, commiserates on this emotional conundrum we've all found ourselves in at times throughout our careers.

While Chad doesn't tell the guests in the group how to overcome their emotional hurdles (I jump in and quip that this is what people pay me for), he does give some straightforward career advice that I believe is worth repeating.

"There are 4 channels for finding your next job," he says, "Job postings, recruiters, your network, are the first three. The last one is blazing your own path."

Chad tells the attendees that the job post applicants face the most amount of competition and the least amount of empathy.

Either you match the profile or you don't. Don't take the rejection and lack of follow up personally. In the nature of this game, it's a statistical crap shoot. It's the least personal, but there is some small statistical evidence making this route worth taking.

Second, Chad says, are recruiters - meet as many as you can, have as many working for you as possible, and find the recruiters who specialize with specific companies and industries. Build relationships with these individuals and be open to them even while you have a job. For the specialized folk, recruiters are the way to go as they have access to people you'd otherwise have to pay to meet.

Third, is your network. "Activate it," Chad says. Let people know you're out there, what you want, and keep reaching out. "If you don't have a network then build one on the site (Malakye.com)," he instructs. This is where your sales skills come into play: invite people to help you and build relationships as a friend and as a professional. There will be many doors that close in your face; keep knocking.

Fourth and, "Where there is nobody competing against you," according to Chad, "is your own path. Research who you want to work for, learn as much about them as possible. Get your hit list of your top companies and keep knocking until you get in."

I chime in and say, "In other words, become a stalker."

The joke breaks the tension. "It's true," Chad insists, "Learn as much as possible."

Chad encourages people to go after what they really want, to go places that nobody else dares to go, and to give themselves a break when things aren't so great. He speaks with time-worn experience.

"I'm a salesman," Chad says, "That's what I do here at Malakye... I've heard 'no' more a lot but you've got to keep at it until somebody says 'Yes.'"

In a genuine and heartfelt manner, Chad intimately understands what Malakye community members go through. And, while acknowledging their personal struggles, he reminds them what Malakye strives to do: connect people, to remind everyone who is looking for talent that, as their slogan proclaims, *We Are Here.*

"Don't connect with just the recruiters here today," he says, "Connect with each other." A subtle reminder that we're not only in the market for a job, we're in search of new business partners, trusted colleagues, and - if we're lucky - friends.

After the Shmooz had ended I animated with my hands on my chest, "Wow, Chad, that was some real heart to heart there in the group today."

He looked at me with a tilted smile and said with a breath, "It was like talking into a mirror."

Call me sentimental, but this is why I believe in what Malakye does for job seekers and why Chad does what he does. There are lots of job sites out there and we all use them. However, none of them have the founder and owner facilitating events telling you IRL* that the struggle is real all the while encouraging you to trust yourself as you choose your own path in life. He doesn't harp on how great a product Malakye is - he simply says to use the site as one of the many tools you'll use to make your dream career a reality.

There was nothing magical about what Chad Mihalick said in the Shmooz career strategy group discussion that day. However, inspired by the individuals working their way through that room, I'm inclined to believe that if we apply those words of wisdom to improve our attitudes and mix it with the community building platform that Malakye offers then career magic is simply bound to happen. I know it is for me.

*IRL = in real life

Questions to Ask Yourself:

1. How have I employed the four channels to a new career opportunity?
2. Am I aware of the tools and resources available to me in my career?
3. Have I focused on my emotional development during my career development?
4. Do I allow myself to be vulnerable so that I can share what's really on my mind?

Recovering After Job Loss: the Forgotten Phase of the Job Hunt

Let's discuss the period after being fired and laid off.

It sucks. It's painful. Especially when you didn't want to be let go.

Separation stings on so many levels because it can leave an emotional impact long after we've severed ties with our former company.

The Separation and the Fallout

Getting fired or laid off is tough and the mental mindfield is the first hurdle to tackle before heading back into the job market.

Even if you saw the separation coming from a mile away, nothing can quite prepare you for the shock of hearing that your work experience is over. It feels like you've been led out to pasture or worse, taken behind the barn and shot like Old Yeller.

There' the emotional fall out:

- Feeling totally lost
- Disenchanted
- Angry
- Hurt

The plethora of emotions catches you like a whirl in the white water.

Then, you retreat to lick your wounds and sentence yourself to exist amongst the living dead until you can snap out of the funk.

The thing is, everything you need to know in order to get back on the career track is within you.

It's just buried under the junk (negative thought processes and self-sabotaging behaviors) that has got us down. It's all inside and it's all around - but we're getting ahead of ourselves.

Getting Over the Grief

One of the essential steps of getting back into the job market is getting over any sense of grief, loneliness, and even betrayal that you may feel.

This process involves treating yourself with kid gloves. This is a period to nurture yourself through the uncomfortable parts of job loss to adequately emotionally prepare for a new professional experience.

Many job seekers make the mistake of hopping right into the job search either for a lack of funds or out of fear.

The tricky thing about hopping right into the job search is there is a tendency to go into job searching with a "get anything" mindset.

That "anything" might be the exact opposite of what you really want. But, for the sake of personal enlightenment, bear with me…

Taking the time (whether it be a concentrated weekend, a few weeks or months, or even a year) to resolve inner conflict can help you get into the right frame of mind for the job hunt. Taking time to reflect and resolve doesn't have to be drastic like hiding in a monastery or going back to school. It can be as simple as going to the beach or park to connect with nature just to get out of a work setting and into the bigger world.

Feeling grounded and connected to what's important to you at this phase of your life reveals actionable goals as a result of this period of self-reflection and contemplation.

Connecting with Others Once Again

Once you feel grounded and connected, you can begin gently connecting without friends and network to get into the mood of socializing.

Networking can be a draining process which is why I recommend filling up the emotional bank first before making withdrawals.

Reviving your spirit is essential so that people can get a sense of your confidence about your job hunt instead of feeling pity for your job loss or doubts about your future. In other words, when you're not reeling from a job loss you're confidently working on expanding yourself to embrace bigger opportunities. And thus, others are confident to help you out.

Recovering from a job loss is a natural part of the job search process, but often goes ignored.

I have seen this happen during the 2008 financial crises and some are still living with the trauma of getting laid off because they haven't properly worked through this essential phase.

Don't get stuck in the past. Give yourself time to blossom and be patient with the process. It takes a lot of courage to trust again.

Remember, the answers to your next career move ultimately lie within and around you.

You just have to see them with a fresh pair of eyes.

Don't rush the recovery process because it's an essential part of the growth towards the next big thing. Nurture yourself. When you're ready you'll get the inner feeling that the job hunt is well under way.

In fact, taking the recovery time to heal after a job loss means the job hunt has already begun.

Questions to Ask Yourself:

1. What does my inner wisdom say about how I feel and think about my lost job?

2. What does this pain or discomfort I feel about my job loss tell me about how it all went down?

3. Do I have a friend or coach who can listen to my side of the story? Can they give me a positive perspective?

4. How can I treat myself compassionately as I grieve my job loss? What are my energizers?

5. Once I have given myself adequate time and care, what is the one challenge I'll take on as the "new" me? What would the old me have not risked at the old job?

Your Job Search: Effort and the Goldilocks Effect

When it comes to effort, the Pareto Principle says that there is an 80/20 rule: 20% of effort creates 80% of success.

And, when effort comes to job hunting, there are two types of effort that are communicated throughout the process:

1. Physical and mental effort
   and
2. Energy obtained as a result of the work done.

Take a moment to observe your own schedule and analyze what you're doing with your time.

It's easy to judge the effort you put into your job search as a waste of time when rejection is a likelihood. This paradigm alone is enough to discourage anyone from putting their authentic self out there.

When it comes to your job search, how do you measure and know for sure what efforts create the most long term value?

I think of effort as the Goldilocks Effect. Based upon the old fairy tale, too little effort and you won't have enough energy to get where you need to go. Too much effort and your focus gets scattered and your energy burns out. Just enough effort - now that's where the "luck" happens.

When job searching, there is a tendency to get caught up in the fear of missing out. "*FOMO*", as the kids call it. FOMO creates an instinct to shoot at everything with a shotgun approach. Any whiff of opportunity and *kablam!* Just throw yourself at any and everything and hope there is a result from your efforts.

"*Nobody can say I didn't try,*" I've been told time and time again.

I've recognized this attitude at Shmooz events and with my own clients: I've been approached with hundreds of resumes chock full of skills, talent, and experiences and yet, no actionable focus.

There is a hope that I'll understand their past for them; This hope then is transferred to the HR professionals who receive their resumes.

Our efforts and consequently our resumes must answer the following questions:

> *Who am I?*
>
> *What am I doing?*
>
> *What was all of this experience for?*
>
> *What do I want to do with it?*

These questions examine your efforts and put them into perspective so that new opportunities may be inspired from them.

Without a sense of understanding as to why you're spinning your wheels, all of that effort occurs in vain and is ultimately ignored (think the proverbial *File 13*). When presenting yourself on the job search going back to the two types of effort as a calibration of the 80/20 rule can help.

When looking at your professional past and current endeavors, ask yourself these questions:

1. What did I gain/learn/take-away from my efforts?
2. How much time and what kind of effort did I commit to those results?
3. What clear story or message do the two aforementioned answers communicate?

You do a lot each day at work and while everything adds up, a surprisingly small percent of that effort makes a big difference.

Your job and responsibility is to know and understand that putting in the effort is not anybody else's job. You have to figure out what you want and what you can do. Don't leave it up to hiring managers, friends, and your networking partners. And when you can accept that, it becomes easier to get the job that allows you to do more of that good stuff that makes our careers *just right*.

Questions to Ask Yourself:

1. How much mental/physical effort do I put into my job search? Not enough (weak resume and online profile), too much (overloaded with everything I've ever done), or just right (highlighting that work that defines my success)?
2. Does my online profile/resume answer the following questions: Who am I? How did my efforts achieve results? How did that effort define my "brand"?

3. When looking at the proportion of rejection and acceptance in my career thus far, how did the rejection help me to focus my efforts and how did the acceptance help me do more of what I love to do?

4. What activities (at work and on the job search) do I do that provide the most value to others? What does that tell me about how I spend my time?

5. Does my profile demonstrate a concentrated effort or am I scattered? Given the results of my efforts, how can I build upon those things that provide the most value?

Please Don't Tell Me You're Passionate, Tell Me What You're Feeling

Whether I am at Shmooz events or in my office, I often hear one phrase uttered out of the mouths of job seekers more than I care to hear.

That phrase is, "I'm passionate about…"

"I'm passionate about…" could mean a million different things and just about every time, the phrase falls flat because it's void of emotion. It's unfortunate that, during the job search process, we've torn away the emotional component from what could otherwise be a powerful introductory phrase.

Passion is an expression of emotion.

When I'm sitting face to face with someone who, in reality, is desperate to get a job and hardly passionate about anyone and anything else - it shows. When you're at this point, don't tell me you're passionate. **Tell me how you really feel.**

Tell me about the helplessness you feel.

Tell me how disconnected from your deepest desires you feel.

Tell me how disconnected you are from everyone in your life because you've got fears and insecurities standing in the way.

Tell me how you're frustrated that the key people you think can help you to get ahead have let you down or have blown you off.

Tell me how you're totally confused about your future because you're not even sure of what you want beyond getting a job to make ends meet.

Tell me about all of these experiences because *that's* what you're passionate about - you're just not aware of it.

Some of you might say, "This is absurd of me to say during my job search! Nobody will hire me that way."

Believe me, you're saying it - indirectly. Because you can't tell me what you're passionate about besides *"surfing, or making products, and leading people"* and the good old stand by cliche, *"Being the best,"* when I can clearly see your inability to articulate your deepest desires and inspirational forces. I can see that your attention - and your interests (therefore your passion) - is somewhere else.

I've seen enough people in all my years of coaching to recognize where your attention is directed.

Just own up to the insecurities, the fears, and call them out instead of living in denial, trying to convince yourself (and others) that they're not there. Stop saying that it's everybody else's fault when what you're really saying is, "I don't know how to help myself."

The thing is - it's perfectly acceptable to not know how to help yourself sometimes. What doesn't work is expecting the wrong thing to fix your mental and emotional blocks.

Even if you were to get a job - even the *dream* job - it wouldn't fix your deep-rooted fear of, let's say, ageism. You'd start looking for it the second you got on the job. And, 9 out of 10 times you'd find it - because that's where your attention and energy (read: passion) are directed.

So, work through what's really bothering you. Sit down and tell me what's up. Don't tell me, in a rehearsed, beauty pageant form, what you think you're passionate about when I can clearly hear and feel the incomplete answers and see your internal conflict. If you can't see the solution - it's because you're not looking in the right direction.

Working on eliminating the blocks is the very process that'll reveal your true passions.

And, when you can recognize your passions, the chances are, I will, too.

Questions to Ask Yourself:

1. What problems do you enjoy solving? When times are tough, how do you show up to help yourself or others?

2. What are your fears about joblessness or financial insecurity? After listing them, identify how you can deal with them head on.

3. What conflicts keep presenting themselves to you? How would things be different if that conflict was removed? Allow this response to show you a strategy for resolving that conflict.

4. Do you feel comfortable with expressing your fears and inner conflicts? Share them with someone you trust.

5. Do you avoid your feelings when you're going through tough times? Will you allow emotional resolution to show you solutions to change your present circumstances?

Giving It All You Got When You Don't Know What "It" Is

You sent out your resume to a bunch of businesses and hunted for hours online.

And yet, you don't seem to hear back. The frustration level is at its maximum because you don't know what more to do to please these hiring managers.

What gives?

That's the perfect answer.

Wait. Perfect question, you mean?

No.

The answer is, "*What gives?*"

When you're job hunting, you're in the process of giving: your attention, resources, and time - maybe even blood, sweat, and tears!

I've heard a thousand times, "What more can they possibly want from me?"

They.

"*They*" are the individual hirers who ignored your calls, the company, the job market, the economy, the country, and the world - and then, finally *life*.

What can *they* all possibly want more of now?
What could I possibly get from all this giving?
I'm running a business, not a charity!
This is where mental focus and emotional energy is misdirected.

You have a lot to give, but not without a lot of expectations. Expectations can get you down in a way that you're so focused on an expected outcome that you can't see the experiential opportunities that could be better than what you think you want.

I hear many groans. You ask, "Is it too much to get back what I gave? Golden rule and all?"

Absolutely not, but you could be losing out what you really need by blocking it with so much expectation.

I've heard clients say, "I'm just hustling for a job. I just want enough to pay my bills."

So, they spend all this energy and get just that - enough to pay the bills - and nothing more - to keep doing what they've been doing. You're just feeding the machine, but not getting any reward. And, they come back with self-doubt and blame (using the "*they*" word) wondering why they can't get the opportunities they see in their mind and can't organize their mental, emotional, and material faculties to express it into their world.

Focus on what you *really* want to experience. Not just the goal. Setting big goals is easy. It's identifying the purpose and joy of each life experience that is mystifying to most.

Instead of, "I want enough money to pay my bills."

Choose instead, "I am open to the resources to meet my children's needs and help my clients to fulfill their goals in a way that we *all* profit."

The first statement is limiting. You put all your resources and steps into that first goal and you'll get just that. Just don't be disappointed when you get what you asked for.

The latter statement examines your motivations (children's needs, clients' goals) which are bigger picture and can be fulfilled by more than just money. Your creativity and consciousness ramp into gear. The second sentence says that everybody profits. It means we all experience what we put in *and* take home what we all need.

In short: specify your purpose and be flexible with how you achieve your goals.

Look at What You Have to Give and Achieve Beyond the Measurable

The downtrodden look at what's limiting and scarce. Doing this mentally separates you from everything you desire.

If you believe that job hirers are just looking to take up your time, make you work to get a job (yes, you do), and all to just cast you aside, you will enter into every experience expecting this treatment. The prophecy is all-too eerily self-fulfilling.

However, if you look at the process as an exploration, the chance to be authentically you, and an opportunity to expand on and learn more, then you'll get something out of it - even if you didn't get the job.

Sometimes, failed job interviews are opportunities to learn things. Like, "Gosh, that kind of work environment is not for me."

Or, "I learned to stand my ground in negotiations."

Or, "Next time I need to come prepared."

These lessons expand you and in no way does the experience limit you. Unless you allow it.

Purposeful Giving Leads One to Act

Act on what you put clarity of vision and purpose on. Act on the new wisdom you've gained (even during periods of perceived failure).

Acting is building motion: acting in mindfulness of what you really want to enjoy in each experience with the information you've gathered along the way will create your unique career path.

Keep giving your job attainment strategy your best attitude. You're going to get more than just a job, if you're focused enough to recognize the opportunities.

Questions to Ask Yourself:

1. What are my expectations?

2. What new life and career experiences would I enjoy? What have I enjoyed in the past that I would enjoy again?

3. Do I have a positive attitude about my job search strategy? Am I more frustrated than I feel progressing?

4. What have past undesirable experiences taught me about what I really want out of my career?

Make Your Own Luck: How to Prepare For Job Interviews

Job interviews can wreak havoc on self-confidence.

It's exciting to think of a new opportunity on one hand, but stressful knowing that you'll be evaluated by strangers on the other.

What can you do to make an interview go from two individuals looking across a table at each other to looking towards the future together?

Job seekers need more interview advice than the same old brush your teeth, show up early, and don't be a kook and play cool stuff that can be found anywhere on the internet.

Interview luck depends mightily on preparation. Are you ready?

In the words of Rob Dyrdek, "*Make your own luck,*" and in the words of Oprah, "*Luck is when preparation meets opportunity.*"

So, let's ask the questions that'll prepare you to seize your next opportunity.

When I coach job seekers for interview preparation, I ask three main questions:

1. What do you know about the company?

2. What do you know about the job?

3. What do you know about yourself?

What Do You Know About the Company?

When I ask about the company, we're going deeper than where they are, what they make or do, and what they have to offer employees. I am talking about understanding the company's values, their overall mission, and goals; Goals can be long term and short term and can include financial, product, market, logistical, cultural, and other strategic goals.

Additionally, take a look at the company in relation to their competitors to better understand where they stand in the market. You want to know what are the company's present strong and weak points, what makes the company special in relation to others, and what are their present notable initiatives.

Questions to Ask Yourself:

1. What are the company's values or important ideals?

2. What are some of their strategic goals that would explain why this position is open?

3. What do I know about the company's recent financial or product performance? Are they struggling or thriving?

4. What makes this company and products special compared to its competitors?

Knowing about the company and their specific needs, values, and goals helps demonstrate a deeper understanding about the issues they face. Interviewers are impressed to see candidates who know their stuff and it makes getting down to what's important - you and the job - faster and easier.

What Do You Know About the Job?

Once the research has been conducted about the company, get a bit more perspective on the position itself and why it's so important.

Doing so will help you identify the issues that the person occupying the position must tackle and the type of person they need to fill it.

Which will take us to the next question, *"What do I know about the job?"*

Most of the time, you can find out what there is to know about the job in the job listing, but the information you really need to know goes deeper than what's on paper and it's your job to find out what it is.

What are the *real* issues that this position is facing? It's up to you to do some digging by researching newspapers, websites (like Malakye), industry related organizations, friends who work there, and anyone who has insider knowledge.

Also, by asking about the job itself, you can decide if it's right for you and if the partnership between you and the company will be a right fit in the end.

Questions to Ask Yourself:

1. What is the purpose of this role? Has the role evolved since it was initially created?

2. What are the core responsibilities? Goals and objectives? What are their timelines?

3. Why are they hiring for this job? Is it a new role? Did someone move on, get fired, or couldn't get the job done? What's the real answer?
4. What does this job pay or offer in relation to similar jobs in the industry? Does it meet my needs personally, professionally, and financially?

Knowing about the job is key to interview success because it shows that you understand the specific needs that you can fulfill, which makes it easier to sell yourself. After all, the goal of the interview is to get the interviewer to imagine you are already at work, even if you've never done the job before.

What Do I Know About Myself?

Tell me about yourself is most often the dreaded interview phrase.

This question essentially asks you to share what your journey up to this point has been and how it has brought you to the interview moment. I can't tell you how many students and professionals I've worked with that give a deer in the headlights stare. Have hope! It can be answered with finesse!

A lot - and I say A LOT - of people ask me why it's so important to know about themselves during their job search.

Knowing yourself is everything. Knowing what you want out of your life and career, how the company can benefit from your specific offering, knowing what you need to be happy and do your best at work (environment, culture, salary, benefits), and so forth.

Asking some simple and powerful questions can help you understand yourself in relation to the work that you do and it makes convincing someone to hire and pay you what you deserve that much easier.

Questions to Ask Yourself:

1. How does my short term job search fit in with my long term career strategy?

2. Why do I want this job? (Beyond our inner caveman saying, *Me want job! Me want money!*)

3. What are my key transferable skills and on-the-job experiences that I can offer?

4. What are the benefits of hiring me (instead of the other 500 applicants) for this position?

5. What are the gaps or weaknesses that I have to explain? How can I explain them for my benefit?

Pulling It All Together

Preparing for an interview with the right questions takes you from uninformed to empowered.

Every job and every applicant is different, so answers will vary from position to position and person to person, thus making the process of researching and developing your awareness both a mind expanding and fascinating process.

It's possible to be unable to find all of the answers to these questions during your search.

These unanswered questions can be great to ask interviewers, which takes care of the "Do you have any questions for me?" part of the interview. Having questions for interviewers can make you seem more insightful and considerate to the multidimensional aspects of the job.

At the end of the day, when you know about a company and where it stands, you have greater insight about the job you're interviewing for and its ultimate purpose. And, when you are aware and confident about what you have to offer, you can easily make the connection between their needs and demonstrate why you are their ultimate solution.

With some preparation and the right opportunity, you will have known you have succeeded in making your own luck when the interview transforms from a simple exchange of information to an action-oriented conversation that has your interviewer imagining you already at work saying, "When can you start?"

Build a Winning Portfolio For Any Job and Industry

When putting together a portfolio, it's natural to look at our old work with a groan and say, "What can I possibly do with this mess of information?"

No matter what your level, trade and industry may be, anyone can assemble a compelling professional portfolio that can land you your dream job.

Having designed and taught a course on professional marketing material materials to international MBA students at INSEEC Business School and consulted a variety of professionals, I know that it is indeed achievable for all professionals, regardless of trade and industry, to tell a compelling professional story.

Freedom: Unleashing Professional Possibilities

It can be overwhelming to look at the task of organizing all of your past experiences into a logical and cohesive story, let alone grasp the overarching statement that describes your career and illustrates the direction you aspire to move into.

Breath!

When people look at their experience and the idea of a building portfolio, some imagine themselves shackled and chained to their past, afraid that by putting down their experience into hard copy they'll just be attracting more of the same.

Not so!

There is actually a lot of potential and freedom in building a portfolio because it helps to see and understand where you've been in order to develop a sense of direction for where you want to go next.

And, through the process, you can identify:

- The patterns (those you want to continue and those you want to break)
- The growth (lessons you learned and challenges overcome)
- The creative potential (how you can use what you've learned to create something new) in your unique body of work

Perspective: Telling The Story as a Fly on the Wall

No matter the type of trade or experience, organizing the artifacts (images and case studies) can be overwhelming.

Try taking on a different perspective on approaching this task: relive the experience objectively by stepping outside of yourself and re-imagine the experience as a fly on the wall.

Removed from the emotional attachment of the experience, you can then objectively look at what happened from the beginning to end and tell the story from the perspective of a third person.

This way, you can approach the experience from all angles by telling what happened from a variety of perspectives:

- Who was involved?
- What were the core issues and problems?

- How did we (ourselves/team) come to the solutions?
- How did this particular case study affect other departments (such as sales and product development) and stakeholders (customers and clients)?
- What were the core lessons and results from the experience that I took away as a professional?

Inspiration: Developing the Main Theme of the Portfolio

The best portfolios have a theme.

Either the theme is centralized around a core idea (working with a specific spirit or vision for the future) and/or profession (the same job title or reorienting for a different one).

Either theme allows you to get more of the same type of work or help reorient you towards new goals such as a career or job change.

Usually, the theme comes as an AH-HA! moment at the end of assembling and telling the story.

I've heard the theme articulated in a variety of ways.

For example:

- "Oh, all this time, I've been working towards this specific career path all along."
- "I've been striving for driving technological innovation in this industry."
- "This is the type of problem solver/creator/leader I am."

I totally get that some readers will hesitate to say that they've got a pre-planned, consistent theme amongst their collection of work, but there is, believe me.

It's about getting meta and looking at the spirit you put into your work. Your theme can be as simple as designing innovative and life changing products, orchestrating the best talent to create the best human resources, or creating paradigm changing stories through marketing and communications.

It's that consistent passion you bring into your work on a daily basis that serves as the theme and whatever feels right to you is most likely the winning theme.

Building the Future: Getting from Here to There

After having shifted through the gold and the forgettable, illustrated the professional journey through a different perspective, and cemented the whole body of work with an overarching theme, the overall portfolio is ready to inspire the intended reader to imagine how they just can't possibly go forward without you.

Once everything has been assembled, it's time to go back and write the summary page based upon the highlights of each experience. By highlighting how you've overcome challenges and adversity with positivity and forward thinking, in addition to nurturing your career with care and focus, you're able to inspire readers to think of ways that they could benefit from your talents.

An excellent portfolio demonstrates:

- Prioritization
- Areas of focus
- Long term career "nurturing"
- A positive attitude
- A fierce self-determination throughout all experiences

And most importantly, a great portfolio bridges the gap from where you are and where potential clients/employers are and takes you both into the future together.

Questions to Ask Yourself:

1. Break down each experience: What are the key challenges that I overcame? What were the skills, lessons, and experiences that I gained from the problems? What were the end results for the client/company? What measurable outcomes did I/my team achieve?

2. Am I trying to get more of the same kind of work or a different kind of work with my portfolio? What is the goal of this professional marketing tool?

3. Looking at each experience individually and then collectively, are there any key highlights from each that demonstrate a common theme? What is the overarching story I'm trying to tell?

4. Does my portfolio inspire the reader to envision me at work with them?

Why Networking Is a Party

Party time, excellent!

Find out why networking during the job hunt can be seen as a party and how you can socialize your way onto the dance floor and land your next big break.

Express Yourself and Come as You Are

The most important principle of networking is expressing yourself freely with a clear understanding of your talents and overall message to the world.

For this task, you must take responsibility. You can't control who "gets it", but you can control your work and what you say.

With free self-expression, networking isn't a shotgun approach. A one-size-fits-all message doesn't suit everybody.

Have you been to a party where, with a beverage in hand, you go around the room talking to people?

Have you noticed that you just don't vibe with some people and, after a while, try to awkwardly sidestep away from them?

And others you laugh and talk with for the rest of the night?

Let's call the party *life* - and in more specific terms, the job search.

There are moments during the job search party, where you find yourself alone, standing in the corner feeling sorry for yourself. Eventually, you force yourself to get over your insecurities and start introducing yourself to everyone. Sometimes you click with others (professionals) and sometimes you don't.

There will be at least one or two people at the job search party who you click with and will want to work with you, too, because when it comes to networking, the first question you ask yourself is, "Who can I trust?"

However, the second, and more important question we should be asking ourselves is, *"Who can trust me?"*

The principle here is to go into the job search party introducing yourself to everyone you can, but understanding that not everyone will be receptive to what you have to say and that does not mean you're being rejected or that there's something wrong with you at a core level.

It takes a lot of guts to stop trying to please everyone and focus on your goals, your strengths, and your vision. To see yourself clearly is a mental and emotional feat that not all people commit to accomplishing, but when you do it makes it easier for the right networking partners to see you in your truest light - and that sets the foundation of trust.

Finding a Dance Partner: Getting Pointed into the Right Direction

After joining the job search party, you eventually get out of your head and into socializing and talk with different kinds of people (those you click with and those you don't).

The music is blasting and it's time to dance; a moment where you really put yourself out there! People start to pair up and get to groovin' and you feel nervous that you're not going to find a partner - in this case, a job.

But, lo' and behold, the friends (networking partners) you made at the party point you in the right direction saying there's a person (a job or career) standing at the punch bowl, looking for a partner, too. You lock eyes, make a silly gesture, laugh, somebody extends their hand, and off to the dance floor you go… and thus the dance (new opportunity) begins.

Maybe, you and your dance partner will fall in love and be together forever (a career). Maybe your affair lasts only for a few months or years after meeting (a job), or perhaps you just dance for the song or for the evening (freelance).

None of that matters as long as you're engaged in the moment and supported by your friends and enjoying your dance partner's company.

When it comes to networking, think of it as a party where you put yourself out there to everyone, but knowing you'll make key connections with just a few. And, when the time comes to find a partner (a job or career) and observe yourself looking around the room (the job market), trust that your friends will point you in the right direction.

Sometimes, others can see opportunities where you can't and networking is the perfect way to see things with fresh eyes.

So, join the party, be yourself, and trust that those who get you will help point you in the right direction.

Expect the unexpected miracles of networking!

Questions to Ask Yourself:

1. Who in my network trusts and sees the real me?

2. Taking responsibility for my professional image, what am I saying? Is it true to me?

3. While being myself, am I consistently kind to everyone (even conflicting personalities) I meet? Do I try to please everyone?

4. What are 3 strengths or areas of focus that I can easily mention while networking?

5. What perspective can my networking partners offer to help me see myself and job search in a new way?

Job Offers: How to Maximize and Negotiate Them in Your Favor

So, you took up the gauntlet that is the job search: you've lived the highs and lows, gone through the mental and emotional wringer of networking and interviewing and now you've been presented with an offer.

The question is, "What happens now?"

Stick with me to find out.

Having worked your magic, you've managed to manifest your dreams into a new job opportunity. Now that an offer is on the table, most people breathe a sigh of relief and let their guard down.

Not so fast!

Be strong just a little bit longer so you (and for the sake of your loved ones at home) can assure a positive outcome.

Accepting a job offer isn't like throwing a coin into a wishing well, hoping that your requests will be heard.

Whether you've clawed and scratched your way up through the internal "food chain" or battled your way through hundreds of applicants, now is the time to ask for and secure what you are worth and negotiate a contract that both parties can accept.

Balancing the Give and Take

The employer and you have to balance out the give and take.

Employer wants to offer you a certain amount of compensation for an expected amount of work done in a specific way for specific results. For example, you might be compensated six figures to travel a lot for business, work over 50 hours per week and for the personal sacrifice of not being with your family. You're giving the employer a lot more than work and travel. You're giving memories you won't make with your family.

Are you willing to accept this arrangement?

Before accepting a job offer, be crystal clear in your sacrifices and contributions in exchange for the financial compensation and prestige a certain job or company may offer. Some people value their family or personal time more than the financial benefits and therefore reject offers that are not aligned with their life goals. That's perfectly OK and makes room for other employers with different arrangements.

The point is: accepting an offer must be an act that coincides with your values and priorities.

Negotiating the Complete Value Package

The second key part of accepting a job offer is negotiation.

Negotiation is an important step toward cementing the work relationship and establishing a "covenant" of understanding.

From all the years I've coached managers and executives, I can tell you that many companies low ball on their first offer and applicants who are so desperate to end their jobless misery will accept the first offer.

It's a trap!

I'm not saying that most companies are wrong or bad in this approach. After all, if you could get a bro deal and save 20-30%, you would, wouldn't you? There is a difference between a value exchange and exploitation.

Keep your eyes on the prize.

Go into negotiations knowing your market value. That is, know how much a company would pay for your unique skills, knowledge, and performance. And, know how much it would cost to replace you.

Would it take one month or one year to replace your expertise? If you don't know, do some comparable research or ask a recruiter in your field to help you figure that out.

What is the cost of living for you and your family? What do you need to earn to buy or rent a home, car(s), education for children, gas, utilities, and other expenditures for living? Do the math and be sure to think about taxes, too.

Then, consider the perks offered by the company. What are the perks and other types of compensation that the job offer lists? Some examples include paid health insurance premiums, educational opportunities, HSA accounts, retirement accounts, profit sharing, company car/phone, products, discounts, free lunches or snacks, sponsored vacations, and discounts at local businesses and associations. The list goes on, so be sure to tally up their value, too.

Once you have considered Part 1) the sacrifice for compensation and Part 2) actual compensation and you have done the math, you can go back and negotiate a contract and compensation package that works reasonably for you and your new employer.

Be realistic but be bold. They'll either accept or try to wiggle into something that's in line with their needs and budget. You might have to go another round of negotiations, but hang tight - it's doable!

Ensuring Your Goals Align with the Offer

Finally, have the wisdom to accept an offer that fits within your short and long term plans.

Both the company and you are presenting opportunities; the job offer is a part of the entire conversation.

Ask yourself, "Am I accepting something that's right for me? Are the personal sacrifices for compensation worth this exchange?"

If so, accept the offer and move forward. If not, tactfully decline and orient your attention towards someone else who can help you realize your goals.

One of my bragging rights as a coach is that my long term clients, on average, earn 20-30% more with every new job offer they accept.

You don't need a straight poker face like mine during negotiations, but you do need to conduct some preparation and reflection to ensure you're being fairly compensated for your sacrifices and contributions to make your work worthwhile for everyone.

When you feel like you are valued, you are more committed and willing to do the very best jobs possible. The first place to recognize *how* you're being valued is in the job offer.

Questions to Ask Yourself:

1. Is the initial job offer lower than discussed during the interview process? What will my counter offer be?

2. Have I done adequate research on my value (knowledge and performance and replacement cost)? What do I know and what does my research tell me about my worth?

3. Does the job offer meet my financial needs to ensure my lifestyle is adequately supported? Why or why not?
4. What are the perks offered besides salary? How much are they worth all together?
5. Does the work contract fairly compensate me for the personal sacrifices I will have to make? If not, what needs to be negotiated in order to work for me?
6. Am I willing to accept less for the prestige of working in a well-known company? Why or why not?

CULTURE

Culture Eats Strategy For Breakfast

Culture eats strategy for breakfast.

Quote attributed to Peter Drucker, the father of modern management.

If there is anything the action sports industry is known for, it's the culture.

It's a culture that builds a business around breaking boundaries and taking the unconventional route to the top.

While all companies employ basic business principles, it's a company's culture that sets it apart and brings its brand spirit to life. Which leads me to examine why employees make their career decisions based on culture and how company culture affects the bottom line.

Understanding Culture and Strategy

When examining company culture, start by defining culture and strategy.

Strategy is the directives that are put down on paper: what goals and objectives the owners or board of directors proclaim from their proverbial mountain top and what executives carry down for their managers and subordinates to carry out.

Company culture, on the other hand, is the spirit of *how* the work gets done and *how* its people behave. They're the set of values that remind employees what is important, maxims that simply express a rule of conduct, and the attitudes that set the tone for every decision that's made and for every conversation that takes place.

Case Study - Losing Culture through Acquisition

Despite how well meaning companies can be, company culture can get lost in the numbers and, in this case, happened during an acquisition.

In the case of Luke (name has been changed for privacy), he made his exit from a family owned and operated skate company shortly after it was acquired by another brand because of the stark difference in company culture.

He cites his departure from a creative, collaborative culture to playing a numbers game focused only on the end result.

Luke says, "You went from asking ourselves, '*What's new in skateboarding*?' to 'How *many units can we sell?*' and 'What *are other guys doing?*'".

Recounting his experience, Luke says how he felt the difference immediately:

> We obviously did something right for the company to be bought out. The company was making millions and the employees knew how the company felt about them. Suddenly, employees felt disposable and I couldn't see myself there anymore. The company was no longer

filled by cool people who wanted to make cool shit. There was no personality and passion anymore.

Luke goes on to explain why company culture ultimately affects his career decisions:

> Employees' priorities are changing. I'm a family man and I am not going to just quit like that, but I am passionate about what I do and hope that it shows in my craft… company culture drives my career choices… you can feel it in your work environment when the culture becomes stale. From what I've seen, I'm aware of that and I won't be the type to ride the wave because it's a nice paycheck.

Syncing Culture and Strategy

Strategy and company culture *can* and *do* go hand in hand and when in sync, they drive clear growth initiatives, inspire teams to develop products that resonate with their audiences, and originate relatable stories.

A syncable company culture entices top talent and, even when team members come and go, the spirit remains the same making forward progress possible. Additionally, clear values that establish the foundation of a supportive work environment are reflected in the benefits and perks the company offers.

When culture is dysfunctional, talent performance struggles, products fail to sell, and messages get lost in the noise. Dismal financial figures are results of these factors. Some companies manage to pull themselves out of their own hot mess and correct the attitudes and behaviors before it's too late. Many, however, fall by the wayside and into obscurity.

Asking the Important Questions

Where do you go from here?

Good strategy starts by asking better questions and coming up with truthful answers that become part of an endless process of self-evaluation.

Can you think of your own?

Questions to Ask Yourself

1. Does our culture reflect our values? What are they and how do we employ them?

2. What is our maxim? Instead of a wordy and confusing mission statement, think of a short, easy to remember phrase that any employee - from the bottom up - can remember, like "People before profits."

3. What are our consumers saying about our culture?

4. What kind of environment are we creating? Do our benefits and perks reflect our values?

5. What is our general attitude in solving problems? What is the tone of our conversations? Are we holding ourselves accountable for mixed messages?

6. Do our employees know how the company feels about them and how do they feel about us?

Three Qualities of Authentic Leaders

During my years of coaching a variety of professionals, I've noticed leaders possess many common characteristics.

While the debate as to whether authentic leaders are born or made will rage on for a millenia, I can say that having these common characteristics can make an inspiring leader - whether or not you're called "Boss."

While there are many qualities of an authentic leader, these are my top three:

- An everlasting willingness to learn and grow
- A desire to create independent teams
- The ability to put the ego aside

When managers start working with me, they are obviously involved for their own reasons and have their own self-interested questions, like:

- How can I better manage my people so they quit eating up so much of my time?
- How do I get people to respect my authority and ideas?

- How can I get my team to work together and stop complaining?

These questions are natural because they help managers do their *own* jobs so *they* don't get fired.

However, as coaching progress continues, I've noticed that the questions go from the theme of *"How can I help myself?"* to *"How can I help my people?"*

The Will to Learn and Grow

Natural leaders, and even those who need a little coaching, are people who possess a willingness to learn and grow.

Everyone comes from somewhere. Everyone is born into this world knowing nothing.

Even great business leaders like Richard Branson, who is dyslexic and performed poorly as a student, named his company "Virgin" at the suggestion of an employee because he was new at business.[8] Branson had to grow and learn to achieve his dreams.

What separates those managers who crash and burn from those who thrive is the willingness to take on new ways of thinking and acting - even if taking on new ideas challenges everything they know to be true.

Willingness to learn and grow is so important because it's vital to adapt to changing demands and business paradigms. This type of mental and behavioral agility comes from a place that accepts our present limitations and focuses on ways to break through them.

---

[8] Losing My Virginity by Richard Branson

The Desire to Create an Independent Team

While talking with a veteran HR pro about the subject of leadership she said,

> The ultimate compliment for me as a leader is when I leave for two weeks and nobody even notices that I was gone. It means that I've trained my team to do their job and others' jobs so well that they are leaders, too. It's that need for control and hiding information that dooms many managers.

The sign that a team is not independent is when all projects stop when the "leader", or more classically known as the micro manager, isn't around.

If the leader is not communicating or insists on being involved in decision making at every step, then work stalls and the performance of the whole team slips.

My clients who have successfully gone on to manage stellar teams respect their employees' intelligence and skills. They guide their team towards self-management and decision making instead of micromanaging their every move.

Quite simply, leaders have the power to create new leaders.

Putting the Ego Aside

Many business leaders and managers have a tendency to get caught up in the attention, power, and control that their position affords them.

Unfortunately, when out of balance, the need for these things cause poor communication, micromanagement, distrust, and a plethora of other management woes that destroys any potential for an effective team.

Let's face it: we all have self-imposed limitations.

Having the self-awareness to acknowledge self-imposed limitations and deal with them (either by strengthening them or hiring someone who is stronger in the area) involves putting the ego aside in order for the whole team to move forward.

Examining our own areas of improvement and taking a global perspective to the meaning of progress is a key element in authentic leadership.

Putting your ego aside doesn't mean not accepting rewards and recognition when they are due to you. It simply means reframing your perspective from a place of self-interest to mutual fulfillment so that global needs are met.

Who Leaders Are and Why You Need Them

The lone person on stage in front of hundreds of people talking about goals, and visions, and lofty ideals is a common image many people have about leaders.

The truth is, most authentic leaders are in the trenches, have average intelligence, have known more failures than successes, don't have a billion dollars in the bank, and are unknown to the vast majority of the world. And yet, authentic leaders still manage to influence our world in a positive way.

Authentic leaders have a special influence on people in a positive way. Authentic leaders spark the desire to learn and grow and inspire people long after they're gone.

Questions to Ask Yourself:

1. Does the phrase, "Do what I say and not as I do," reflect my management skills? How do I lead by example?
2. Do I manipulate people with fear or control or do I get them to think independently to solve a problem?
3. How do I positively inspire change in my work environment?
4. Who was the best/worst manager I ever had? What was their management style?
5. What objectives do I need to meet? How do my employees help me meet my objectives? How can I help them help me?

Behaviors of Memorable and Influential Leaders

How does one touch the hearts of others and in effect, make themselves memorable and influential leaders?

This question has been explored by marketing research companies for decades and debated by some of the world's greatest philosophers for a millenia.

You easily remember the products and people who touch your heart.

For better or worse, we are sentimental creatures. By examining the word sentimental from my other language, French, I see the words senti (from sentir, meaning to smell, taste, and feel) and mental (from mentale, meaning mind).

As sentimental creatures we recreate memories in our minds through reliving the emotions and sensations we originally felt.

Navel Gazers: Striving to Relate

Professionally, we get so caught up on making our own ends meet and surviving through the career food chain that it's easy to make every interaction about ourselves:

- *What can I get?*

- *How can I use this relationship or opportunity to get me to the next mark?*
- *How is someone taking something from me?*

We're all (from time to time) navel gazers. Caught up in this deafening loop of self-centeredness, we lose sight of our relatability and how we make other people feel.

First, take a look beyond your own belly button and ask, "How relatable am I?"

Striving to achieve common goals is one of those workplace catchphrases that everybody throws around, like loyalty, commitment to the team, blah, blah, blah. They've been jam packed into every leadership development workshop that they no longer provide any depth of meaning.

Relate means *to be brought back* and *to be connected to.* Can you safely say that you're relatable to others in the workplace? If not, then you've lost their hearts and minds.

Nurturing Hearts: Generating Good Thoughts and Feelings

Creating memorable connections within the business context is all about nurturing hearts and minds.

After having taken a cold, hard look at yourself as a leader and realized how you may have succeeded in watering down the words and concepts of leadership (such as loyalty, teamwork, vision, and innovation), you now have to nurture those hearts and recapture their minds.

While you can't be in complete control of *how* people remember you and the values you stood for, you are in control of what you put out and the amount of effort directed into building rapport.

I'm not talking about getting people to fall in love with you - *although that would be nice* - I'm just talking about meeting people where they are at, honoring them, and working mindfully to assure that what you say and do evoke the most empowering and positive feelings.

For example, you may be passionate about some work projects and not so much about other projects.

You go on crusades to influence employees and colleagues to take up your passion projects, too, and make the fatal mistake of ignoring their passions and what's important to them.

Honoring others isn't a bleeding heart, self-martyring, bootlicking concept.

Honoring others is about just saying, "I get what you're going through. I may not know what your exact experience is like, but I know the feeling."

This simple phrase can snap out emotionally and mentally numb navel gazers and can, at first, capture their attention.

Seeing the Opening: Creating Memorable Moments

Now that you've got their attention - it's possible to influence with integrity and go forward together - the process of nurturing their heart has commenced.

Once a person realizes that you recognize how they feel about certain aspects of their work experience and how they perceive their work, together, you can bring them into your world by identifying the feelings, issues, and thought processes that resonate best within them.

Nurturing trust and rapport is an essential step towards building positive psychological associations.

Go back to a time when someone has said to you, "I feel you", "I hear you", or "I see what you mean."

These cues are little signs that help us know that we're connecting on an emotional level. These moments allow you to express, during another person's most receptive moments, your own feelings. The result is emotional rapport.

Making the Connections: Building Rapport and Creating Influential Moments

You don't have to be a social scientist or a great spiritual master to be a memorable and influential leader.

You can:

- Call B.S. on your own bad attitudes and self-centered behaviors.
- Meet people where they're at emotionally and mentally.
- Be open to making meaningful, *heartfelt* moments.

Anyone who tries to separate emotions and feelings from work is dead in the water.

Your passions are what drive you in the workplace and if you can't relate to what others are passionate about and appreciate them, then the chance of nurturing hearts is lost.

Think of a great boss or colleague.

Did you smile?
Did you laugh?
Did you get excited or feel confident?

This person has succeeded in being memorable and odds are, they have inspired and influenced you to think, do, or believe in something by *first* relating with you on an emotional level.

When I ask my clients to remember someone, they immediately go to an experience that evokes an emotion.

To effectively lead, convince, and encourage employees, interviewers, and colleagues you, as a memorable leader, must:

- Evaluate your own intentions
- Meet others where they're at emotionally, and
- Create moments that nurture emotional rapport

Try these methods for yourself.

You just might be surprised as to how memorable and influential you really are.

Questions to Ask Yourself:

1. Do I relate emotionally, not just logically with my teammates and subordinates? Do I really know how *they* feel about things?

2. Do I put relatable emotion and heart into the concepts I preach? Do I separate feelings and logic?

3. Do I put in time to not just establish, but build rapport within the team on a consistent and personal basis?

4. Do I notice how often my employees talk about how they feel, see, sense the world around them? What sensing words do they use on a regular basis?

5. Thinking of a great boss and a horrible boss, what are the feelings and experiences that separate the two? What techniques and behaviors did they use in building/blocking rapport?

To the Moon: Building Winning Teams

Teams are more than a mere assemblage of people and talent.

Teams are an ethos that drive direction towards a common goal.

Each part, or function, of a team moves and flows in harmony with the others.

An example is the Apollo 11 NASA space shuttle design.

The intricate team of designers and engineers with special and unique functions had one mission: get safely to the moon first and win the space race for the U.S.A..

People come and go. And so, the team is constantly evolving, occasionally disrupting the group dynamics for better or for worse. A shared vision of excellence, repeated and spoken, has to be acknowledged by each person of the team every time someone leaves or joins.

For example saying, "X person left, so let's continue to work together in a Y way in order to meet Z goals."

This simple communication maintains focus on team spirit in the face of changing group dynamics. The result is fostering an equilibrium of overall function towards a common goal.

In team management, surmounting the temptation of the "blame game" is a constant battle of ego for each individual member.

Instead, leaders must make the choice to absorb the shocks of mistakes and failures and encourage its members to ask themselves, "What can we do as a team to avoid individual and/or group mistakes in the future?"

The dynamics of the team therefore goes from "to each his own" to "all for one and one for all."

Going back to the NASA example, if just so much as one part of the shuttle or its calculations are incorrect, an error could spell certain death for its astronauts or costly delays.

While your team might not face this kind of astronomical pressure, the concept that the group's success is greater than the sum of its parts remains true.

"Who am I to be my brother's keeper?" you might ask, "It's already exhausting enough to do my own job at a satisfactory level!"

Fair enough.

However, consider this: one part of the supply chain goes down and all other areas screech to a grinding halt.

The manager who knows the jobs (and issues) that his or her team members face have more perspective and success in the long term.

There is no wonder why Americans admire leaders who have worked their way up in their career. These individuals know the value of each contributing function and see all jobs as an integral part of the whole.

While you might not have started at the bottom of the food chain, you as a leader have to remember that teams don't serve to simply support one person at the top. Teams collectively support the whole.

Compassion, a word seldom used in business, drives the intention of the group as internal dynamics are considered and directed outward toward the consumer.

Your problems are my problems are our problems, one could say.

Fostering a team ethos is a job for bold leaders; leaders who are not satisfied with complacency.

Steve Jobs once said, "It doesn't make sense to hire smart people and then tell them what to do; we hire smart people so they can tell us what to do."

You can be a special kind of team leader who can adopt a trusting and empowering attitude. In hand with a collective recognition of group responsibility, facing internal and external challenges is achievable.

Whether it's the moon or a quarterly target, unwavering focus and consistent collaboration can help a team make its mark.

Questions to Ask Yourself:

1. Does our team have a clear mission? What is it?
2. Is my team harmonious or counter productive? That is, do we let old, bad habits get in the way of our work?
3. Can members of my team trust me enough to confide their issues and do they believe that I will answer their questions or support their needs?
4. Do I/my team make the priority to be receptive to any glitches in the framework of our team dynamics? For example, do I actively support others in my team who are overwhelmed?
5. Do I provide my team creative ways to express themselves? For example - anonymous messages, forums, questionnaires, group brainstorming, etc.

Can Your Team Work without You?

Can your team work without you?

You went on a much needed vacation and got a little R&R.

Now that you're relaxed, recuperated, and hopefully got a healthy glow, it's time to get back to your team.

The great part about vacations is getting away from it all - especially the mental atmosphere of work.

Thinking about returning to work isn't so much about the work per se, but the delight or dread of going back to the team's dynamics.

If dynamics weren't grand before you left for vacation, odds are things will be just as dysfunctional upon your return. The responsibility falls upon you to use the opportunity of freshly vacationed, sunglass tan lined eyes to understand how your team functions with you around.

Maximizing the Moment of Your Return

The moment of your return is the opportunity to see who pulled through for you and held up the fort.

It doesn't take but a few hours to figure this all out. Odds are, someone will happily report all of the drama and updates to get you up to speed. Look at the first morning back as seeing what happens when the smoke of your foggy perspective clears: are things dysfunctional or are they in shipshape?

Returning to the office isn't just an opportunity to see who's done what (or nothing at all). It's also an opportunity to access your own management and leadership skills and to clearly observe the roles and the dynamics that are truly at play in the workplace ecosystem - for better or for worse.

Like cream and fat, your temporary departure can churn up conflict and reveal the best and the worst of our people skills and the quality of your professional relationships.

Actively listen to everyone. Uncover the different versions of what occurred during your absence. Use this moment to develop critical thinking and non-judgemental observational skills. And, use this moment to understand the ways you work and the attitudes you hold.

Even with the foreboding prospect of discovering some interpersonal bugs upon return from a great vacation, do not be dissuaded from leaving next time to enjoy your well-deserved personal time.

With a new perspective, you're simply getting to the core of the operations and the relationship dynamics that affect the overall emotional and mental environment you expose yourself to and help shape.

Returning from vacation is an excellent opportunity to benchmark the overall health and well being of the team so that you don't have to anxiously dread coming back from vacation the next time.

Questions to Ask Yourself:

1. When I come back from vacation, what are the first things that I observe (through the successes and challenges experienced while I was gone) about the relationship dynamics of my team? Positive and negative.

2. Can my team operate without my being at work? Have I trained and helped ensure operations are steady and reliable?

3. Who were the key people who stood out in positive and negative ways during my absence? What can I learn from their performance? How can I ensure more, or less, of that behavior?

4. Judging by the performance of my team, what skills can I improve in order to empower and harmonize my team?

New School & Old School: We're All Learning

There isn't much compassion that goes around when we think of the multigenerational workplace.

Compassion means *to suffer with* and when it comes to the multigenerational workforce, there's a relational gap in between the "new school" and the "old school". A relational gap exists because we know well the trials and tribulations of our age group, but not that of those who have come before us, let alone those who will come after us.

Believe it or not, we're all in the same boat of career challenges - and, more importantly, even if we're not conscious of it, we all go down together when the going gets tough.

I'm not going to say to the younger generation, "Oh, respect your elders, because they're wiser." Just because someone gets older, it doesn't mean they get wiser with age.

However, the road of learning is a two way street on which the teacher is also the student. In other words, no matter if you're 20 years younger or older, we can all learn, share, and teach each other something of value. That this exchange is what defines the learning process. At every age, we're the student and the teacher.

Here's why:

Now, there are those older professionals who've been around the block, been knocked around a few times, and still have the wind in their sails.

They give the attitude that makes us say, "Man, wherever they're going, I want to go there, too."

Young professionals don't have to wait to be an old, salty sailor to sail the tides of change: you're already doing it with the rapid change of trends, technology, and globalization.

Some older professionals get stressed by rapid change and worry about their ability to keep up (mentally and physically). This is the chance for younger professionals to become teachers in their own right, by exchanging their practical knowledge for the wisdom of the mentors.

In my case, I freelanced with an ad and creative executive 20 years my senior. It was fascinating to work with her because, while I knew the trends and tools, she had spot on insight and savvy business skills. Our exchange was exciting and motivating because we both knew there was so much more to learn. I brought in the new technological opportunities and she brought in her practical wisdom - it was, for me, a match made in work heaven.

Within each of us is inner wisdom that lies hidden until we can learn to connect and express it with each other.

With a certain degree of consciousness of our own and the other generation's limitations you can overcome the boundaries, such as prejudice and agism, that stand between people. Because, at the end of the day, we're all traveling down the same road of professional life - some further along than others and some who know the way better than the rest of us. Who knows what kind of magic can happen with the intention to work together peacefully and harmoniously.

Questions to Ask Yourself:

1. Who is the person who has a lot of wisdom in my work environment (age not being the deciding factor)? What message does their wisdom consistently say to me?

2. Knowing that I'm a teacher, too, how can I be a positive representative of my generation?

3. Is there someone of a different generation that I could be of service to? How?

4. What are the prejudices that I hold onto that affect my ability to relate to colleagues of different ages and backgrounds? How do these prejudices no longer serve me?

5. Can I think of a time when someone older or younger taught me something new? What did that experience tell me about learning?

The Logical Fallacies of Layoffs

Unwanted necessity. A last resort. A necessary evil in the world of business.

These are some of the labels that justify the choice to layoff dozens if not hundreds, or even, thousands of employees.

These phrases do not do the justice of adequately expressing the amount of incompetence that goes into mismanaging a business.

As blunt and ugly - and even polarizing - as this statement may be, it is up to leadership at all levels to admit to the follies that leads them to believe the surest way to growth is through eliminating those who are poised to support it.

This is not a statement about keeping outmoded and redundant jobs that machines and younger professionals exiting school can do in a shorter, more efficient amount of time.

This essay is focused on using layoffs as an excuse and method for justifying business moves to satisfy short term margin requirements on a balance sheet for a small group of investors.

"Cutting back" is not a justifiable tactic for poor resource allocation and unrealistic earnings projections.

Layoffs, even during "tough markets" are symptoms of two things:

1. Insufficient long term growth strategy (and)
2. Unrealistic expectations

Both are in the hands of leadership and as such are a reflection of those in charge at all levels from chairman to the manager on the shop floor.

Growth doesn't happen by magic. Growth happens as a result of building culture and a long term strategy built around that culture.

Fundamentally, layoffs are counterintuitive to these two things and say A) I don't believe in the future and B) The culture doesn't matter.

One might argue that layoffs are simply removing the bottom tier performers: the "weak links" and the "hangers on".

For the sake of argument, let us consider for a moment that this is indeed true. However, those who do remain - the best, the brightest minds - are not blind to the statements that culture doesn't matter and nor does long term growth. Before long, these agents of change, savvy on business trends, will assure an unprecedented brain drain by leaving for other businesses with better cultural prospects.

And, so what? Leaders who justify these measures argue, we can always replace human capital - it's being born anew everyday!

That, too, may be true. However, a repugnant reputation has already been formed and talent with any inkling of self preservation will avoid the short term, reactionary culture that now reeks from every corner of such an enterprise. In short, the long term consequences of layoffs are not soon forgotten.

Industries are built by those with long term vision; a collective of individuals brandishing the torch of commitment to excellence. Reactionary thinking makes businesses dispensable, especially when there are other businesses with more qualified leaders to carry an industry forward. Buying and selling talent is no longer a one sided endeavor of a bygone era. Higher educated professionals have more choices now than ever and will select those companies worth investing their time and energy in and who reward that kind of loyalty.

Layoffs are fundamentally public relations disasters that say more about leadership than any sort of logic that can attempt to justify it.

The questions that glare the unflattering light of truth bear to reveal incompetencies in business acumen and people management. For those who can answer the following questions before "resorting" to layoffs, they will not only save their reputations but also assure creative thinking in problem solving.

Questions to Ask Yourself:

1. Who are we laying off? These are people, not positions to move around like pawns on a chessboard.

2. What measure of performance do we risk to lose and gain by their removal?

3. Is the layoff strategy long term in thinking? What is the fundamental message (e.g. the truth) that can be easily understood about this vision at a shareholder and public meeting?

4. Are we attempting to satisfy our hunger for short term gains? Do we risk impoverishing our overall health by

starving ourselves of talent who eventually will not play fool to our maneuvers?

5. Who remains amongst those we have fired? What reward do they receive for their loyalty: an unexplained sense of job insecurity? A job for tomorrow, but not for the long run? What is the best answer to offer our best performers?

6. How long do we, executive leadership, plan to stay aboard? Are we selfishly playing the game to hedge margins in our favor as a way to entice buyout for a short term payoff? Do we really believe that this strategy will go unnoticed?

7. Is our performance and leadership decision to lay off a reflection of sound business decisions and are our strategies "coincidentally" timed for when we are about to leave the company?

Having answered these fundamental questions, and assuring that there is no element of doubt, dishonesty, and selfishness on the part of those executing this plan, we can then access the business choices that led up to this "solution" and discover where things went wrong and finally address them.

If poor character is ruled out, then incompetence must be considered.

What does he/she not know that leads to drastic measures?

If these individuals cannot be trained to avoid such failures, then they must be replaced by those who are capable.

For, out of all the accounting that gets done to justify layoffs, responsibility is the last thing to be taken into account.

Coincidence?

I think not.

BUSINESS ETHICS & PROFESSIONALISM

Communication 101: Follow Up to Follow Through

Have you ever found yourself midway through a project and the person who was supposed to help completely fell off the grid?

You notice that time goes on and still no follow-up?

Irritating, isn't it?

One of the biggest complaints my clients have is a lack of follow up from others.

Communication is a two way street so it's best to work on your own communication skills first than to wait for someone else to get back to you.

What Is Follow Up?

Follow up is a communication and leadership skill that often goes neglected and under-exercised.

Follow up is the act of remaining committed to a goal until its completion. Follow up is achieved by clearly updating or closing conversations so that all parties involved can take away a mutual understanding.

Sounds simple enough, huh? Not always.

Follow up can either be the fuel that keeps work going or the door that closes so that others can open.

When used constructively, follow up keeps others informed and demonstrates that projects are properly handled and progressing, if not concluded.

Proper follow up shows consideration for our relationships and for others' time, acts of kindness, and resources.

Follow up, as a behavioral tool, maintains focus and keeps relationships on track (or properly concluded).

Follow up can imply, *"Enough of what we were doing before. Let's change speeds or stop this completely."*

Why Don't People Follow Up?

Failure to follow up happens for a variety of reasons:

- You intend to respond but get so buried in your work that we forget.

- You don't have the answer to what someone's asking us and rather admit ignorance, you ignore requests instead.

- You don't want to help people out because of some conflict of interest and don't know how to say no so you hope the conversation dies out.

- Some highly specialized individuals lack the social skills to properly respond to communications or notice cues.

- Or, just don't care about how your actions impact other people.

Whatever the reason, it's your responsibility to get over your hang ups, awkwardness, forgetfulness, or rudeness and follow through with people.

It can be unpleasant to say no or confront someone, but it's better to get over the hump and to face the issue than to make the matter worse… and be forced to deal with their consequences later on.

What Happens When You Don't Follow Up?

When you don't follow up with others, you can throw projects off their course and send mixed social signals. Not only that, it appears rude, arrogant, and inconsiderate of others' time and situations.

The operative word I hear is, "Douchey."

Others can interpret a failure to follow up as self-centeredness which communicates a "what's in it for me" attitude, leaving people feeling frustrated, angry, and even confused by a lack of communication.

There are very few excuses and reasons to justify a lack of follow up and, more often than not, excuses make things worse than make them better.

How Can I Ensure I Follow Up?

Timely follow up is key.

As soon as you receive a note, get more news, make progress or learn of any problems, it's your job to let others know what's happening on your end. It's tempting to procrastinate, but then the opportunity passes or the acceptable time window closes and then things get awkward. Then, the time comes to explain why you dropped the ball.

Just follow up as quickly as possible. Follow up doesn't have to take much time – just a few minutes, at least – to continue or finish conversations.

Mutual understanding is the fundamental purpose of follow up and is not about being a slave to emails and the whims of others.

When it comes to updates, either positive or negative, context trumps content because the focus isn't entirely on what's being said as how and when. Focus more on the timing, the general attitude of the message and allow the facts to speak for themselves.

When it comes to a tough project or situation that has slowly progressed, give others a heads up so they're not left wondering what's going on.

If you are disturbed by a rude email, phone call, or text, it's ok to take some time to cool down and think about ways to respond politely and constructively. But wait too long and it shows that you're sulking. Choose to do and be better than the default of doing nothing or too little.

Remember, the point of following up is to either create endings or make steady progress that everyone can clearly understand.

Your own lack of follow up says more about you and your ability to handle issues than the situation at hand. When done right and practiced regularly, following up is an essential skill to resolve problems, maintain strong relationships, and communicate yourself clearly and respectfully.

Questions to Ask Yourself:

1. When was the last time someone left me in dead air in the middle of a conversation or project? How did that make me feel and affect me? What perspective do I have now as a result of this experience?

2. How many projects have I been a part of that have stalled or just completely stopped as a result of a lack of follow up?

3. How time sensitive are my communications? When does my input expire before others move on without me?

4. What keeps me from following up (procrastination, awkwardness, confusion, lack of clarity)? What do I need to do or know in order to move forward?

5. How important are my relationships to me? Do I follow up and show that others matter to me?

6. How can I clearly and succinctly follow up without having to constantly go back and forth?

Stop Being a Slave to Email

I coach managers who get at least 100 emails a day.

CEOs have reported at least 150 a day.

When we do the math, that's at least 30,000 emails per year.

I've been told, on average, that it takes one entire work day (8-10 hours) a week to answer and organize emails alone. That's at least 400 hours spent each year working on emails.

During my coaching sessions, general housekeeping (answering emails, making phone calls, and dealing with recurring tasks) always comes up and I am asked the following common questions:

- How do I better manage my time?
- How can I deal with this overload of requests and questions and actually focus on long term projects?
- How am I supposed to improve my performance when I'm constantly on my cell-phone?
- How can I unplug and decompress from all of the demands and refocus?

Email management is relatively a new phenomenon.

With the advent of smartphones (think Blackberry phones being notoriously called Crackberries) answering emails became no longer reserved for the first thing in the morning after a nightly break. Now, with company provided phones, managers and executives are chained to their smartphones – and within the context of international business and differing time zones- email management is a non-stop job.

Getting a constant barrage of emails takes a mental, emotional, and physical toll.

There's the mental concentration element, the stress of dealing with a variety of conflicts and miscommunications in a delayed format, and the physical consequences such as carpal tunnel, neck and eyestrain, and headaches. There is also the personal conflict of answering emails in front of family and significant others during private moments.

It's not enough to understand the challenging context and consequences of email management. Managers and leaders must manage their time resources wisely enough to keep it under control.

I've worked with quite a few managers that have a compulsion to answer emails as they get them and all in one go (good luck) so they can, according to them, have a clear mental state to focus on other housekeeping items and projects. The problem with this is that this is not how emails work. They come in constantly. Many (just about all) that I've worked with even answer emails at home and in the middle of the night and in bed. I won't go into how this is a bad time management habit....

Prioritize Emails

When working with clients, I ask them to prioritize their work and assign time limits to each project and task in order to challenge themselves to stay focused. Part of that work is email management and one method involves putting it off as long as possible.

- Sort through the emails at the start of your day.
- Star or flag is absolutely important and must be answered right away.
- Put a different marker on those that can't wait until the end of the morning (before or after lunch) and another marker on what can wait one-two-or three days.
- Work on what needs to be answered right away and go on to other work.
- If it's possible, set up a time or time frame at different parks of the day to work on lower priority messages.

Schedule Your Server

Another email management tip is to set your server to push emails every few hours or during a set interval. This way, the flow of emails is trickled in through bunches, rather than in a constant flow.

Train Others to Write Better Emails

When working with subordinates, ask them to wait to send low priority emails until a certain part of the day and wait until they've got all the facts or questions they need until sending an email in order to minimize the number of emails in an effort to consolidate messages.

Be sure to teach subordinates and others to know when to call, use slack, stop by your office, and when to write.

Turn Off Email Indicators

To deal with the psychological compulsion to answer emails, I recommend turning off the email indicator and email sound notification on your smartphone. So that, while you're in meetings, working at your desk, on the road, or on your personal time, you're not emotionally compelled to answer emails.

Email management is a skill that takes practice, commitment, and emotional control.

In essence, develop and maintain the self-discipline it takes in the face of constant, around the clock, demands for your time and attention.

Play with the techniques above and think about creating your own email management techniques to make emails a part of your job, not your entire job.

Questions to Ask Yourself:

1. Are my email habits taking up too much of my time and attention? Do my friends and loved ones complain about my answering emails during personal hours?

2. What new habits can I try to minimize the time I spend looking at my phone or email?

3. Who sends me the most e-mails? How can I educate others to better write emails so they can get better responses from me? Can we discuss them quickly in a meeting or by phone instead?

4. When can I focus on emails and how long can I wait in between checking/answering messages?

5. What needs to be answered by e-mail and what other topics/issues can be answered through other means?

6. Do emails cause me to feel anxiety, dread, or worry? Why?

Conducting Yourself During Business Trips

Whether you're new to work travel or are an experienced globetrotting pro with thousands of skymiles, there are major benefits to traveling with class (not just business class). Whether you're flying the friendly skies, traveling on a train, or driving to different domains there's much to learn when going to different places - and not just in a business sense; a personal and cultural sense, too.

When it comes to business travel, we think about all of the logistics and the stress of traveling, not to mention actually doing your job and there are a ton of other questions to consider, too:

- *Who is going to watch my kids while I'm gone?*
- *Will I be able to accomplish my performance goals in the limited time frame I have?*
- *Will the cost of traveling to see my clients be worth the business I'm going to get from them?*
- *What's my gate, again? Will I miss my connecting flight?!*

Aside from these typical logistical and performance questions, business travel is more than just about getting the job done in another location - the focus is also about how you get it done.

How you build rapport with your traveling companions, foreign partners and clients can make or break how you resolve last minute production issues, communication problems between headquarters and a foreign office, and more. Without getting too much into social sciences and anthropology, let's take a step back and be more sensitive - if not more aware - of the subtle nuances of work travel and how the consequences follow you back to our home office.

Being All Eyes and Ears: Listening and Observing

Listening and observing are some of the most underplayed skills in business travel.

Many go to a client or key stakeholder to make them happy, armed and ready with all the presentations and collateral they think they want to hear and see. *Or,* are determined to fix an issue with a supplier or distributor. Whatever the cause for concern, business travel affords the initial opportunity to just *get there* to really see what's going on; To see what's really happening instead of what you *imagine* is happening.

Listening and observing can also help in building rapport with foreign offices.

As many businesses are globalized, it's common to have branches throughout the rest of the world. While colleagues are under the same company with presumably the same corporate values, the cultural values and social aspects of foreign offices, for example such as those in Japan, may be totally different to the corporate headquarters in the United States.

Paying close attention to the subtle nuances of differing cultural behaviors- dining etiquette, drinking etiquette, after hours socializing and partying, and even dining with a foreign colleague's family - can forge strong professional relationships and mutual respect creating lasting rapport.

Dare to Say Yes

If it doesn't kill you or cause you to commit moral injury, then make the effort to say "Yes," as much as possible while on a business trip.

Building new relationships, changing the outcomes of difficult circumstances, and finding new opportunities in career and life by saying "*Yes*" become the doors necessary to move forward.

For example, my husband Franck was at a tradeshow in Europe. A competitor asked him to join him for a few beers, but he was tired and just wanted to go back to his hotel room.

Franck heard my voice in his head saying, "Say yes. This is an opportunity to network."

They got to talking about their personal lives and goals. And, months later, when an opportunity came up, this competitor referred it to Franck and it helped to change his life and achieve some dreams.

Fulfillment of his dreams resulted from saying yes to the opportunity and building rapport with a person who could have otherwise remained a stranger.

Zip Code Rules: Be Careful of What Follows You Home

Now, saying yes doesn't mean taking on the mantra "What happens in Vegas stays in Vegas".

I could tell you at least a dozen examples from the top of my head about embarrassing stories of clients and their colleagues that happened on business trips.

The moment they leave their zip code, some people think it's an opportunity to totally release their inhibitions, break their moral code, and betray their family and values.

Just for the fun of it and more importantly to drive the point home, I'll tell you one true story…. are you ready?

A few professionals I know went on a business trip to a European country for a global sales meeting. In Europe, the alcohol can flow pretty freely at business events, so a few of the employees got totally trashed and ended up hooking up.

A colleague went back to his room to find that his other colleagues (a man and his ex-girlfriend's mother) were hooking up in *his* room. And, on top of that, they left the curtains open and other colleagues were *watching* them hook up!

When this colleague was finally able to get back into his room to retrieve his belongings, he found the place totally trashed with unmentionable protective devices and bodily fluids left throughout the hotel room. Not only was this particular colleague disgusted, but everyone who was at the sales meeting knew about it and this couple was forever branded at the global headquarters for this scandal.

Long and short of it - have fun while you're on the road, but don't let the shenanigans follow you home.

An Indecent Proposal: Hosting Clients and Colleagues

Many couples, including my husband and I, work as a team to entertain traveling business guests. There are ups and downs to this joint effort, so it's worth mentioning.

This one is a personal and funny story of my husband's grandmother, Grande Mamie, who hosted her husband's business associate and how she dealt with his inappropriate and unwanted advances.

My husband's grandfather sold industrial machinery to champagne houses in France. Occasionally, he would invite business associates to his villa in the south of France and entertain them there. Grande Mamie was responsible for creating a warm and inviting experience that could foster his business relationships.

One evening, Grande Mamie was in the kitchen cooking and this associate started making moves on her, even daring to grab her bottom. Without thinking twice, she slapped the man away and told him that she didn't care who he was and that she wouldn't tolerate his advances. She shut this man down and needless to say, he wasn't welcome to their villa anymore - and his business was no longer wanted.

No matter how tempting it is to hit on your colleague's wife, don't. And no matter how wanted someone's business is, don't let it compromise your values.

Business Travel and Hail Marys

Business travel can sometimes be seen as a Hail Mary to accomplish something that just can't be done at the home base: trying to fix problems, land accounts, establish connections, and build businesses and opportunities that at one time existed only in your imaginations.

For some of you out there, work travel is simply another part of the job and without it, progress simply can't happen.

While business travel has its benefits and disadvantages (I'm sure it's easy for you to think of a few things people sacrifice) there is always something to be gained from the experiences from being on the road. With basic attitudes towards handling how you take care of business either domestically or abroad, you can go the distance for your career and bring the success home.

Questions to Ask Yourself:

1. What is the best part about work travel? What is the worst part?

2. How do I feel about being away from the people and things I love? Do my feelings surrounding separation distract me when I'm away?

3. What do I worry about when I'm working on the road?

4. How can I make the best of working away from home? How can I bring home with me?

5. What fears, anxieties, or worries can I resolve that prevent me from enjoying work travel?

The 3P Plan to Starting a New Job Like an Insider

Whether you've landed a promotion at your current company or are starting a new job at a new company, there is always an element of anxiety about how successful you'll be.

I help companies coach their employees during a process called *onboarding*.

Onboarding is a fancy, human resources term for the process during which a new employee develops behaviors and gathers knowledge to effectively do their job.

I help new recruits focus on the first three, critical months by setting up an action plan that addresses the "Three Ps" - **people**, **priorities**, and **personal life**.

Onboarding is an underestimated, yet important, period because starting a new job can be an enjoyable and purposeful process for all involved.

People: Finding Your Place in the Company Culture

Just as you're trying to get a feel for our colleagues, you're being evaluated from the get-go.

Colleagues are deciding if you're actually any good at what you do, if you'll assimilate into the culture, and if you'll actually make a positive difference. It's nerve wracking to know that everything you do at the beginning will leave a lasting impression on others. This impression affects your work relationships and how well you'll be able to do your job.

Take the time to talk with and listen to everybody you can:

- People you'll be working with directly,
- People you'll be working with indirectly, and
- Even those who don't even work in the same department

Take the time to investigate the true essence of the company culture that wasn't communicated during interviews in order to get a general feel of core interpersonal and operational issues affecting your new job.

By understanding the general vibe of the company culture, the key relationships will start to reveal themselves. From there, you can learn to adjust your approach in order to foster rapport from the beginning.

As enticing as it is to get involved in gossip with the office drama queen, focus on blending in at first and steadily getting a grasp of who you can count on and who you'll need to treat with kid gloves. You might even find a mentor.

Priorities: Prioritizing Tasks and Projects

Hopefully, you've prioritized key tasks and projects with your boss before accepting the job. But, in case they were not totally clear, establishing priorities and objectives can reduce performance anxiety and establish a sense of purpose from day one.

Simply write down a list of key job tasks and priorities.

Maybe, with your old job, you were used to doing things a certain way and enjoyed doing some tasks more than others. But this time around, you're responsible for tasks you've never done before or don't necessarily like.

For example, you've never managed direct reports before and now you have to start coaching them and making sure they arrive on time and do their jobs. Establish priorities with your boss to know how to prepare yourself for new tasks. Doing so reduces the confusion and intimidation associated with taking on new roles.

Also, it's tempting to try to prove ourselves and our worth right away. After all, we want to show why we were hired in the first place, right?

While you certainly may want to get at least one success on the books during your first three months, it's essential to reign in the attitude and the tunnel vision to get projects done at all costs. In other words, check yourself before you wreck yourself!

Once again, establish a focus on key projects, key relationships and prioritize them with your boss. Get their guidance on how to approach the next few months intelligently.

Personal Life: Set Up a Short-Term Work-Life Balance Plan

Managing personal lives when starting a new job is a major stressor for those with families, pets or loved-ones with special needs.

Not everybody gets a new job where they can clock out at a specific, regular time. Some jobs have irregular schedules and can seem to bleed into personal lives. For those who are salaried or are starting new jobs that require a lot of travel during the onboarding process, work-life balance can be hard during the first three months. So, get a plan of action with your personal support network to help out when it comes to caring for loved-ones and other personal needs.

Schedules can be hectic at first and new routines can feel overwhelming. It's normal to feel challenged when going through a career transition.

Spend the first three months observing the rhythms of work flow and daily expectations while allowing that personal support network to temporarily handle your responsibilities. When a rhythm gets established and tasks become more natural, it'll become clearer on how to draw the line between work and personal life and easier to make any necessary adjustments to create a smoother long term work-life balance.

Incorporating the 3 Ps

Creating a three month, 3P plan before starting a new job can calm those first day jitters that often provoke you to immediately latch on to bad habits and negative relationships. With a newfound sense of purpose and armed with specific goals, the onboarding process for a new job can become an exciting growth experience to help you reach new professional heights.

Questions to Ask Yourself:

1. What are the key working relationships that will affect my new job? Does my manager have any advice for me on how to approach them?

2. How much time will I devote to asking questions and listening to everybody at my job? What questions will they be?

3. What are the new tasks that I'll be taking on? What does my manager have to say about their priority?

4. Which projects are of high importance? Which ones can help me get a win within the next three months?
5. What is my personal life strategy while I get adjusted to this new job? Who is in my support network and what are the short term goals and priorities that I need to manage?

Five Ways to Make Working from Home Work for You

The image of working from home sounds intriguing because you can get away from the glare of fluorescent lighting and can fart and nose pick without anybody around.

However, working from home either full time or on flex time can be more complicated than originally imagined, so I've put together five ways to succeed and enjoy working from home.

I've worked from home since 2009. It was simple and much more flexible before I had my babies. There was a period when I watched them full time and worked around their schedule and during the evenings. It was an opportunity to master self-discipline and motivation. Needless to say, I know the challenges of working from home, but I know that it's possible to manage.

1. Create a Reasonable Work-Life Separation

Creating a reasonable work-life takes some decision making.

I have two young children and their care and upbringing are my biggest priority in life right now, so it's easier for me to put off projects and put things down when I feel they need me.

Whether you're working at home with kids or just tempted by cruising the internet or going out to the beach, it's essential to your success to create some reasonable boundaries between your work demands and your personal life demands. Creating separation can include a physical or mental space for working that allows you to shut the door between the two.

Creating a sense of detachment from one "world" to another is essential.

This goes both ways - if you get too distracted by the demands of your home-life, your work suffers and vice versa. If the dishes or laundry is piled up, leave them until a break presents itself. If the kids are whining and the babysitter seems flummoxed, resign yourself to let them handle it. If it's time to be with the family, let e-mails hang until after dinner or when the kids are asleep.

Of course, I say reasonable work-life separation because life and work can get intertwined. People usually come from a place of wanting to do their best for everyone, so we're constantly making choices and compromises based on what is for the highest good and that's where the lines sometimes blur. And that's ok.

Go with what intuitively feels right and give yourself a break when lines are sometimes crossed. Tomorrow is always another day and opportunity to try again at making this work at home experience work for you.

2. Have a Routine

Routines are not just for babies, they're for professionals, too.

Having a routine doesn't mean strictly sticking to a schedule where all freedom and flexibility are gone. Having a routine just means creating a flow that keeps you going in a forward motion instead of melting onto the couch watching random Youtube videos until 11am and suddenly wondering where all of the time went.

If there are regular daily tasks to do, then set a time that makes sense during your natural work and energy flow.

For example, work on projects that require clear concentration before reading emails to avoid getting sucked into mental ping pong with clients or colleagues. Eat lunch early or late and take a quick nap if the need arises.

A routine is simply identifying your natural rhythms that allow for creativity, administration, and communications and building your day around what allows you to work at your most optimum activity levels.

3. Prioritize Projects and Tasks

Prioritization is essential because knowing what comes next keeps the day's agenda, and your choices, focused.

Having a few core tasks to work on keeps the momentum going and it reminds you as to what is important before getting sucked into other distractions. It's easy to get caught up in conversations or meetings, or help another colleague remotely, or even get distracted by the kids or loved ones.

And, for the perfectionists who try to get everything done in a day: having two or three goals for the day can give you the pat on the back we need when realizing that maybe we didn't get the 100 things on our list done like we wanted to do.

4. Set Intentions with Proactive Communication

Proactive communication and follow up is a big part of working at home.

Because people can't see you or walk right into your workspace, they are wondering if you're actually doing your work instead of binge watching a series on Netflix.

A helpful tip for proactive communication is to learn how to clearly and proactively outline the day's tasks and issues for your manager or subordinates. Outlining key tasks sets the day with intentions, clarifies any confusion, and gives a sense of direction and concreteness to what can seem fluid and unclear to ourselves and to others.

If problems arise, be sure to make your distant presence known and let others know that you're either aware of the situation or actively working on it.

5. Employ a Motivational Technique

To stay motivated, some people listen to music or go for a walk, some call on a mentor before working on a project, others play a quick game of sudoku, others pour a cup of joe.

Some might even reward themselves with a small treat when the work is done. Whatever your motivational technique, allow motivators to give you a sense of fun, a small, refreshing change, and inspiration to whatever task you're dealing with at the moment.

I recommend the Pomodoro Technique a lot. Named after the tomato-shaped kitchen timer, it's where one sets a timer for a certain period - say 10 or 20 minutes - and does as much as possible to beat the clock. When the clock finishes, either the work is finished as is or you can step back and take a break for 5 or 10 minutes and then start the timer challenge over again. This simple motivational technique can help give you the impulse you need to take on a challenge and break it into small, measurable steps.

Simply saying that one is working from home doesn't mean that the balance has been figured out.

Creating separation is nuanced, but it is possible and requires a lot of self-discipline and personal insight on developing a rhythm and mindset that works for you.

Whether or not you're a flex timer or a full time home-based professional like myself working at home can be a wonderful way to have a career and balance a personal life.

Questions to Ask Yourself:

1. What are the ways that I can create a separation between work demands and personal demands?

2. What parts of my day can I use to focus on work? On my personal needs?

3. What key tasks or goals each day can give me a sense of accomplishment?

4. How do I feel about managing my routines and my focus? Do I need help to overcome emotional or mental blocks regarding my self-management skills?

5. What are my motivators? How can I make working fun and productive?

6. How can I give myself a break during the day? What are my energizers?

Create a Psychological Safe Zone at Work

Conflict management is often used as a codeword for "dealing with idiots who don't have a clue."

Unfortunately, we've all been guilty of this attitude and it generally bites us in the rear at home and at work.

Emotionally intelligent leaders see conflict management as more than a buzzword on their resume and a mere formality in leadership training. Conflict management first involves compassion and releasing judgements about ourselves and others. Effective conflict management shows that even good people can have a bad idea from time to time.

Create a Psychological Safe Zone

The first practical step in conflict management is establishing a zone of absolute psychological security that says conflict is not only healthy but an essential part of the decision making process.

Emotionally intelligent leaders create a psychological safety zone of total neutrality where saying what is necessary achieves win-win results.

The reason why creating psychological safe zones is so important is that many companies, and more specifically managers, rule by fiat instead of consensus and occasional dissent.

Any whiff of dissent causes even the most well-intentioned leaders to rule with an iron grip, thereby squelching any chance of creative, diverse ideas to take even one breath of life.

Psychological safe zones encourage healthy and respectful dissent. When employees feel safe to express awareness of conflict and even argue bad and unclear ideas, they're essentially challenged to advocate for what is best for the company, instead of misdirecting energies into protecting their own interests.

Striving for What's Right Instead of Fighting To Be Right

By establishing a psychological safe zone, leaders encourage their team to advocate for corporate values and check their own ego at the door of the safe zone.

Strive for what's right, instead of fighting to be right, more simply.

Team members must be able to freely and openly challenge ideas and products that might not be in line with what the company stands for and challenge leaders to better clarify and communicate what could very well be good ideas, but bad explanation or poor execution.

This is also a reminder for executive management to let go of their own egos. The least senior person (and least paid) could very well have the best ideas simply because they're closer to the solution.

Emotionally intelligent conflict management means honoring input from all levels and from all perspectives and judging their impact and value accordingly.

Conflicts Are Opportunities for Decision Making

Conflicts are opportunities and essential parts of the decision making process.

Conflict informs the decision maker what is missing from the equation (either, for example, essential input or more data) and whether or not there is a hidden benefit or caveat to the decision itself (and if the risks are well worth the reward).

Getting Along in the Sandbox

Adults function with adequate conflict management skills and tools - many, not so great.

You can't have Mom handling your sandbox arguments for you anymore. It's your opportunity to learn to resolve conflict intelligently. The good news is, when done correctly positive results are sure to follow.

Questions to Ask Yourself:

1. Is my work environment a safe place to have conflicting ideas and healthy dissent? If not, am I responsible for this problem? Do we let ourselves come up with creative solutions or do we fight for fixed solutions?
2. Do I get worked up when someone disagrees with me? What am I afraid of when it comes to healthy debate? Am I unprepared? Do I lack insight? Have I checked my ego at the door?
3. Do I let the data speak for itself or do I get caught up in opinions? Which matters to me more?
4. Do I honor the process of decision making and allow conflict to have its place and purpose? Why or why not? And, how can I change my attitudes/behaviors?

5. Who has a stake in the decision making? Are they involved in the process? Are the deadlines for decision making established?

How to Survive Performance Reviews and Improvement Plans

Review time is here and the mood around an office can quickly go from basking in sunshine and having spring fever to feeling like a contestant on Survivor with yellow fever.

Companies use review time at the end of the first quarter to do their spring cleaning (read *fire*) and it's high time you took the cue to get organized with a little review preparation.

Spring Cleaning: Don't Get Voted off the Island

At the turn of the new year, you've probably learned about new performance initiatives that you must meet or have been put on a Performance Improvement Plan.

Those first three months you were focused on getting on board with the required changes and implementing them. By now, at review time, you're going to be evaluated on the execution and whether or not you'll progress from here.

Managers and human resources managers employ Performance Improvement Plans (PIP) to weed out weak performers.

In some instances, PIPs can be used effectively with the right guidance and motivation but, essentially, they're used to accumulate written evidence to avoid litigation when it comes time to fire people. If you've been put on a PIP or are facing review - now is the time to get ready to meet the tribal council.

Preparing for a review is all about dusting off your professional image and making it shine.

A performance review is an opportunity to show how well you have:

- Dealt with conflicts and problems
- Exhibit a paper trail of communications
- Demonstrate how you've followed procedures (even if those procedures don't make much sense), and
- Show how you've worked on bad habits and are working on developing good ones

This way, when face to face with a reviewer or boss, it'll be easy to CYA*[9] with strong evidence to confidently discuss your performance.

Building a Strong Position

Instead of walking out of the meeting room with a verbal beating or worse - a pink slip - it's possible to walk out with a raise and a pat on the back. The difference between the two is follow up and preparation.

The key strategy of confidently facing performance reviews is changing your mindset about them.

Instead of thinking, "Oh God, how can I shift the blame to something or someone else to buy me time?" focus on "How can I communicate my progress and contributions?"

---

[9] CYA: Cover Your Ass

Shifting from a place of no control over your circumstances to a place of control over ourselves can change the tone of discussions: from defensive to proactive.

Questions to Ask Yourself:

1. What were the main goals and objectives that I was assigned last quarter? How did I deal with them and what are the results?

2. Who was responsible for putting me on review or on a PIP? How did they help me achieve my goals? How did they not?

3. What were the competencies that I was asked to improve or employ and what was the result?

4. Do I have written evidence supporting my efforts? If so, what does it say?

5. What mistakes did I make? What affirmative defense do I have for them? (Example: Yes, I missed this meeting, but I was handling a client issue at the same time.)

6. What is my salary now? What have I done to merit a salary increase and what evidence do I have to back that up?

7. What are some new or existing goals for the next quarter? How can my reviewer help me achieve them?

The Aftermath: Rebutting Unfair Reviews
Maybe you've already faced a review and it wasn't pretty.

Maybe you feel bruised even if you managed to survive elimination. What happens now?

It's possible to rebut them with some clarity and objectivity.

More often than not, my clients don't know how to respond to negative reviews. They just get disturbed or defensive and don't know how to move forward. Time to go from feeling hurt to thinking constructively.

Questions to Ask Yourself:

1. Did we focus solely on performance (accomplishing the job)?

2. Was I recognized for the specific goals and objectives I achieved? If not, why?

3. Were there any issues that kept me from meeting my targets? Like, maternity or sick leave, redirection of time and attention to other diversions, relative performance (of others in the group), and no prior notice. Were these fairly acknowledged?

4. What are the appropriate channels and methods for rebutting a performance review?

Springing Forward from Q1 to Q2

Now that the first quarter is almost over, you can be sure that companies are using performance reviews and PIPs to do their own spring cleaning and are voting those that aren't strong enough to make it to the next quarter off the island.

Based on the premise that you worked diligently and did your job to the best of your ability in Q1, performance review time allows you to showcase all that you've overcome and accomplished, reflect upon and correct past mistakes, and come up with action plans for new challenges… and, maybe get a raise out of the deal.

With adequate preparation and a clear focus on what matters, review time is just the fresh start you need to stay on job island for another day.

Photo Memories 271

Leslie with friends playing and learning through her surf and marine biology club called Nalu Surf and Ocean Preservation Club during the 2002-2003 school years.

Leslie supporting local North County San Diego surf groups and businesses.

Leslie with Marcelo Bengochea, former CEO of Superbrand and former Creative Director of Reef during the filming of the webseries #Drive.

Leslie with Chris Cote, action sports commentator and Editor-in-Chief of Encinitas Magazine during her filming of #Drive.

Leslie with Larry Balma, founder of Tracker Trucks and co-founder of Transworld Magazines.

Leslie with Allen Carrasco creative President and Director of Carrasco Creative, close friends collaborators for the #Drive web series.

Franck Juvin-Acker, Leslie's first coaching client, during his days of dreaming of working in action sports.

Leslie and Franck Juvin-Acker on one of many snowboarding days during their years in Annecy, France where Franck worked at Salomon Snowboards.

Leslie and Chad Mihalik, President www.malakye.com

Photo Memories 277

Chad Mihalik and Leslie Juvin-Acker teaching a career workshop together at Fashion Institute of Design and Merchandising in Los Angeles, California.

Leslie speaking to hundreds of job seekers during a Malakyz.com Shmooz event in Long Beach, California.

Leslie teaching emotionally intelligent leadership at Agenda Workshop for Group Y in Long Beach, California.

About the Author

Leslie Juvin-Acker is a certified Global Career Development Facilitator who delights in educating professionals and groups emotional intelligence skills. Leslie is the author of *Engineering Your Mood: Feel Like The Person You Want To Be* and became a millionaire using the principles found in her book *The Money Formula: Change Your Relationship With Money In 7 Steps And 15 Minutes Or Less*.

Leslie now teaches individuals from all walks of life to create all manners of abundance in their lives. Leslie is founder and President of Leslie Inc. which provides educational solutions to families and businesses to create happiness at work, in personal finance, and at home. Website: www.leslieinc.org.

www.ingramcontent.com/pod-product-compliance
Lightning Source LLC
Chambersburg PA
CBHW071350210526
45465CB00001B/40